"Steve has done a brilliant job at pulling together a topic that is complex and difficult. He has captured beautifully the importance of church in caring for those who have experienced deep suffering. This book is written sensitively, compassionately and clearly, and shows how the beauty of Christ both challenges our perspectives on trauma and ministers to those impacted by deep suffering."

Karen Sleeman, Biblical Counsellor, Christ Church Cockfosters, London; Visiting Lecturer, Oak Hill Theological College

"When faced with the complex pastoral needs of those who have experienced trauma, we can err either by rushing forward to care for these sufferers without requisite knowledge and skill or by outsourcing all care to secular trauma specialists as if the church has little to offer. Steve's wise and thoughtful book charts a better way. Working from the conviction that Scripture provides the deepest perspective on the experience of trauma, he summarizes current trauma research, builds a biblical understanding of the multifaceted suffering associated with trauma, and demonstrates in practical ways how the church can and must play a central role in the care of those who have endured extreme suffering and its aftermath."

Michael R. Emlet, Faculty Member and Counselor, The Christian Counseling and Educational Foundation (CCEF); Author, *Saints, Sufferers, and Sinners*

"Dr. Steve Midgley tells us that there are two errors we can make regarding trauma. We can think trauma is too confusing and complex and so do nothing to help; or we can be overconfident in our capacity to be agents of healing. If you want to avoid both of these dangers, this book will help you. Midgley provides clear and concise descriptions of the problem of trauma, how it impacts the entirety of human experience, and how the church can be a place of hope and healing. Don't miss the wonderful reflection questions after each chapter and the practical helps in the last section."

Phil Monroe, Psychologist, Langberg, Monroe & Associates; Cofounder, Global Trauma Recovery Institute

T0349390

"A wise and reliable guide for church leaders and members that deeply understands trauma. Steve presents an inspiring and biblical vision of love and care that will bless many. Practical, realistic and achievable in numerous church contexts."

Dr Karl Hood, Lead Counsellor, Melbourne East Christian Counselling Centre; Lecturer, PTC National Centre for Biblical Counselling, Australia

"Even in a small church of 20 people, it is highly likely that a handful of people in the congregation have experienced trauma, the effects of which may still be felt in their own lives and the lives of those close to them. Imagine, then, how many people in your church are affected. The impact of trauma can be isolating and confusing, and as God's people, we have an imperative to provide a place where help can be found and hope can be ministered. I am deeply encouraged by Steve's caring and insightful book and how it will deepen and enrich the gospel care we provide to those among us who have experienced profound suffering."

Laura Perbet, Founder, Grace and Hope Biblical Counselling

"Addressing overwhelming and life-altering suffering, Steve Midgley speaks with a considered, caring and tender voice. With a combination of personal stories and clear theological anchor points, he opens our eyes to the complexities of trauma and then offers us a way forward to care with Christ's gospel of grace front and centre. When I face such things in future, I will do so more thoughtfully and more hopefully because of Steve's insights."

Ste Casey, Pastor, Speke Baptist Church, Liverpool; Author, *I Prayed and Nothing Changed*

"All those seeking to support those who have experienced trauma should read this book. It is biblically rooted, medically accurate and practically helpful. I will be recommending this to all of our missionaries."

Jason Roach, Director of Ministries, London City Mission

"Compassion and courage are both necessary for anyone who wants to care for those who have been disoriented by trauma. Steve Midgley provides both to his readers. The wisdom found in this book will help church members and church leaders understand the experiences of people who have faced severe suffering, and give them courage to help those who are navigating the dark waters of trauma."

Curtis W. Solomon, Executive Director, the Biblical Counseling Coalition

"Steve Midgley masterfully tackles the complexities of trauma with biblical wisdom, offering practical guidance for those caring for victims. His work is infused with the profound hope that both victims and churches long for. This book is essential for pastors, church leaders, and believers who seek to support trauma survivors with the same grace and compassion that Jesus extends to his suffering people."

Darby Strickland, Faculty Member, CCEF; Author, *Is It Abuse?*

"Trauma is not selective; neither is it a new phenomenon. This thoughtful, informative and compassionate book explains the events, experience and effects of trauma and the significant role the church has in responding and supporting those affected. Dr Steve Midgley is uniquely placed in guiding us in this complex area, given his background as a medical (psychiatric) doctor and current roles as a pastor and biblical counsellor. I strongly urge anyone with an interest in trauma-focused care, but particularly those with leadership or pastoral roles within the church, to read this book; I guarantee you won't regret it!"

Dr Rebecca Jacob, Consultant Psychiatrist, Addenbrookes Hospital, Cambridge, UK; Affiliated Assistant Professor, Department of Psychiatry, University of Cambridge

"It takes skill and wisdom to tackle a complex topic and make it understandable and accessible for the average lay person. Steve has done that in this book; with his characteristic warmth and compassion, Steve provides a thoroughly biblical perspective on an issue we all need to grow in our understanding of."

Jonathan D. Holmes, Executive Director, Fieldstone Counseling; Visiting Faculty Member, CCEF

"Our culture is increasingly alert to the reality and impact of trauma, so it is vital that the church becomes more trauma aware. There is no better guide than Steve Midgley. He has combined his expertise as a psychiatrist with his experience as a pastor and Bible teacher to produce a resource that will help churches and leaders become sensitive to others and avoid causing unintentional additional harm through ignorance. Packed with helpful case studies and biblical insight, it is accessible and readable, and should be essential reading for Christians wanting to care well for others."

John Stevens, National Director, FIEC, UK

UNDERSTANDING
TRAUMA

A Biblical Introduction
for Church Care

Dr Steve Midgley

Understanding Trauma: A Biblical Handbook for Church Care
© Steve Midgley 2025.

Published by:
The Good Book Company

thegoodbook.com | thegoodbook.co.uk
thegoodbook.com.au | thegoodbook.co.nz | thegoodbook.co.in

Design by Ben Woodcraft

A CIP catalogue record for this book is available from the British Library.

ISBN: 9781802541373 | JOB-007971 | Printed in India

*In memory of my parents, who would have so loved
to see this book.*

*For my children and grandchildren,
who have brought me more joy than I will ever be able
to tell them.*

To Beth, whose companionship I will ever treasure.

CONTENTS

INTRODUCTION

Trauma captures our attention. And rightly so. The experiences of extreme suffering and the way such suffering can impact individuals and communities is something worth being concerned about—and these things should be of particular concern to Christian believers and to the church.

The sweep of Scripture takes us from the account of creation in Genesis through the fall of mankind and on to God's glorious plan of redemption, which culminates with the renewal of all things in a new heaven and earth. On that journey we see the arrival of sin and suffering, but we also see its final eradication. We live after that arrival and before that ending. Trauma involves an experience of exceptional suffering—an experience that overwhelms a person. Christian compassion—a compassion shaped in imitation of Jesus himself—will cause us to move towards such suffering and pain.

We should not, however, assume that it is easy to do this either wisely or well. Something in us will always tend to pull away from pain. Drawing close to those who suffer makes considerable demands of us, and we will often resist that. Growing in an imitation of Christ is a key part of the way in which self-interest is gradually overcome by self-forgetful love. But while compassion is the foundation of a Christian response to suffering, something more than compassion is needed. Those who want to care well for people affected by trauma need a certain kind of knowledge as well.

Sadly, in our churches, our care has often been less than it should have been. Lacking knowledge or, worse, lacking compassion, we have not been wise in our care of those who have experienced trauma. We have often made it hard for people who have experienced trauma to engage with our churches. Not feeling truly welcomed, they have not felt able to truly belong. For my own part, I do not have to look back many years to see ways in which my lack of understanding led me astray. There were times when I was far less supportive than I should have been toward some whose struggles, I now realise, probably arose from past trauma. Many of us will sense that apologies are needed and that there is much ground to make up. I hope this book can make a contribution to that.

The word of the decade

Thirty years ago, when I was training in psychiatry, trauma barely featured in my training. Trauma studies was still relatively marginal to the mainstream of the mental-health world. Today, studies about the role trauma plays in emotional and psychological wellbeing have become one of the fastest-growing areas of research. In fact, trauma has been described as the word of the decade.

Conversations about trauma are no longer confined to the arena of scientific research. Trauma has become part of our cultural language. This popularisation is such that concerns are beginning to arise about the way the language of trauma is being used. Once simply missing a bus and getting caught in a rain shower can be described as "traumatic", how can the same word be an adequate one to describe the experience of a soldier enduring the worst atrocities of the battlefield? Triggering, flashbacks and dissociation—technical terms to describe post-traumatic experiences—have all entered popular speech. When our culture is using the language of trauma to describe its whole range of experiences of suffering, Christians and churches will need to understand that language in order to engage well.

Why this book?

In writing this book, I have had four central aims.

1. *To engage in an area of important pastoral concern.* In our churches, there will be people who have experienced severe suffering. We do not need to be pastors to feel a pastoral concern for them. The overall responsibility for pastoral care may rest with pastors, but the provision of that care involves the whole church. Every believer should want to care for those affected by trauma as well as they can. Taking time to think about the ways trauma can affect a person will help us to do that.

2. *To summarise secular insights on the experience of trauma.* Because in recent years there has been a huge increase in the study of trauma and the way it affects a person, in Section 2 I have tried to provide an accessible summary of this research. Understanding how our culture thinks about trauma is important if we are going to communicate well in this area. Those who have spent lots of time engaging with people who have suffered trauma will also observe things about the experience that we may not otherwise notice.

3. *To provide a biblical perspective on trauma.* As with most areas of psychological research, trauma studies has developed its own set of technical terms. These are not, obviously, terms we will find in the Bible. In order to identify links between trauma studies and biblical thinking, we need to identify connected ideas which

are used in the Bible. This will allow us to make connections between the language and perspective of trauma studies and the language and perspective of Scripture. I write as one persuaded that the Bible provides the final and deepest perspective on these matters—and, indeed, on everything that really matters—which means that it is through the lens of Scripture that we must both learn from and critique these recent understandings and approaches.

4. *To provide practical pointers toward the care churches can offer to those who have experienced trauma.* It is always important for Christians, and churches, to recognise the limits to their ability to offer care. This will vary from person to person and from church to church. But there will always be a point where wise pastoral carers will know that they have reached the boundaries of their competence. At this point, wisdom dictates that the loving thing to do is to recruit others with more expertise and experience. But before that point is reached, churches can, and should, aim to make a real difference. Even when others with more expertise are involved, churches will still want to do all they can to provide a supportive and loving community.

It is also wise at the outset to identify some of the things that this book is *not*.

First, it is likely that, in places, this book will not be an easy read for people whose own experience has involved severe suffering. It is entirely possible that stories I will use to describe experiences of trauma will, for some, act as unwelcome reminders of their own suffering. It feels important for me to highlight that at the outset. If that does happen, it will make sense to seek support by talking with someone you trust about the issues that it is raising for you.

Second, this is not a counselling manual. It will not equip anyone to provide technical or specialist care. I am not an expert in trauma—it is a field in which I have developed a growing interest, but I have never taken courses in trauma nor have I trained as a trauma therapist. I hope that my coming to this as a non-expert will make this an accessible introduction. I have engaged with relevant literature on this topic and done my best to summarise and explain current theories accurately. I have also tried to do this summarising and explaining in a way that avoids being over-complex or using language that is over-technical. I am aware that this leaves me in danger of falling off either side of that ridgeline. Several friends who have received training in trauma therapies have kindly read early drafts of this book. I am grateful to them for pointing out where I had made factual errors and also for showing me where I needed to revisit sections which were unclear or misleading. Of course, where any such failings remain, the responsibility for them is entirely mine.

Third, therefore, this is not a comprehensive survey of contemporary thinking in the field of trauma studies. That field is too large and is developing too rapidly for this short volume to be anything other than the very briefest of introductions.

Fourth, in writing this book, it is Christian believers that I have had in mind. If you have come to this volume without a faith in Christ then I am, of course, delighted. I hope the exploration of biblical themes and the relevance of the Christian faith to trauma will be of interest to you. I hope it might encourage you to explore the Christian faith further for yourself. However, because I have written this with Christian believers and the church as my primary audience, this inevitably means that I have made certain presumptions about prior thinking and understanding.

For some, what follows will be frustratingly simplistic.

They will notice all sorts of detail that is lacking and which they consider vital. Others, by contrast, will find the material unnecessarily complex and be frustrated by how long it takes to arrive at what they see as the simple truths of the gospel. I have been well aware of both possibilities—you can judge the extent to which I have successfully navigated between them.

Whenever a topic becomes prominent in our culture, it is important that Christians seek to understand it accurately and engage with it wisely. When that topic concerns people who have gone through experiences of severe suffering, there is even more reason to engage as well as we possibly can, and to do so within a biblical framework. I hope that what follows will help us to do precisely that.

SECTION 1

SEEING TRAUMA IN
SCRIPTURE AND LIFE

CHAPTER 1

TRAUMA IN THE BIBLE

Those who knew Tammy well were familiar with her dark moods: the times when she would withdraw and seem both distracted and distant. A measure of hopelessness was always hovering and at times deepened into despair. Both her parents and her brother tried to bring her out of herself, but nothing they said or did made any difference.

Tammy herself might well have told you that she felt as if her life was ruined beyond repair. She had given up hope on so many levels—marriage, children, happiness all seemed beyond her reach. Once she had been bright, confident, outgoing. Now she retreated from any and every challenge. Anxiety would rise easily and recede ever so slowly.

What she hated most were the flashbacks; experiences so vivid that she could physically flinch. They might come from nowhere, especially at night. At other times, a word, a phrase or a touch was enough to bring these blazes of memory crashing down upon her—parts of an experience she longed to forget but knew would now haunt her for ever. It could begin with a feeling of tightness on her wrist, as though strong hands were gripping her all over again. At other times, there might be a vision of the drapes hanging in the room or the embroidered pattern on the bedspread. Even the smell of freshly baked bread—an aroma she had once loved—was now for ever associated with humiliation, violence and pain.

Sometimes she could hear the slam of the door and the silence that followed. Or her own pleading cries—first for him to stop and then, when that appeal had failed, how she implored him not to send her away. When she first realised the wicked way that she had been manipulated and trapped, it had made her angry. But that was long ago, and now she just felt abandoned and alone.

Another snatch of memory was from later that day—of her brother asking questions, speaking instructions. She remembered the way he seemed to take over. Silencing her, controlling her. It only compounded her sense of power-lessness.

The vulnerability she felt in those moments had never really gone away. She was unprotected. Not just then, but now, too. It seemed as if she had become an embarrassment, a figure of shame, despising herself and despised by others. The feelings were so strong and painful that she would do almost anything to shut them out. Were the nightmares rarer on the nights when she drank too much wine? Perhaps. Anything that numbed her heightened senses was welcome.

No one ever mentioned what had happened, but that failure to speak only intensified her sense of shame—the re-alisation that these things were unspeakable. Or was it she herself who couldn't be spoken about? Did everyone think that she was best ignored and forgotten?

Someone had told her once that the king was angry when he first heard what had happened. Yet he had never expressed that to her—there was never a time that he spoke of anger. As for him acknowledging publicly that what was done to her was wrong, and so exonerating her—that had never happened. So, her shame remained. She was a woman disgraced.

Some years later her brother took things into his own hands. "Exacting vengeance" was how he put it. Did he really imagine that more violence would bring her healing? He never asked her what she wanted. For her, it was just one more experience of powerlessness. Another man doing what *he* wanted. She still had no voice. And all that it accomplished was one more loss. She had lost her honour and her hope and now, in the fallout from his actions, she had lost her brother as well.

Desolate

Tammy, as you may by now have realised, is short for Tamar. The man who raped her was her half-brother Amnon, and the brother who took things into his own hands and murdered her assailant was Absalom. The father who did nothing was King David, the father of both Amnon and Absalom as well as Tamar. The whole terrible story is recorded for us in 2 Samuel 13. It's a brief account, stripped bare—rather as Tamar herself was. But the brevity cannot hide the brutality. The aftermath for Tamar is summed up with these few chilling words: "Tamar lived in her brother Absalom's house, a desolate woman" (v 20).

The description of Tamar above is, of course, somewhat speculative. But trauma of the kind she endured will, typically, leave this kind of damage and pain. Feelings of shame and disgrace. A desire to forget and the impossibility of doing so. Flashbacks, nightmares and the fragmented memories that are prompted by sights, sounds and even smells, evoking not so much a recollection of the past as a reliving of it in the present. Those who have lived through traumatic events describe how they re-experience the feelings of shock and helplessness and fear.

Trauma, as I mentioned in the introduction, is an experience that has received much attention in recent years. Trauma studies and trauma research have become a rapidly expanding field. Many new insights have emerged about the way trauma affects a person. There are new theories about the mechanisms responsible for the ongoing impact that people experience, and there are new therapies to try and help those who suffer.

But trauma itself isn't new. It has been with us ever since the fall. Genesis 3 tells of the first sin, with its consequence of God's judgment: spiritual separation from him in a broken world. And before we even reach the end of chapter 4, murdered brothers, bereaved parents and threats of vengeance have all become part of the biblical narrative. Tamar lived in that world, and so do you and I.

Let's consider some of the key aspects of Tamar's experience in 2 Samuel 13.

Violence and threat

Trauma has been likened to a brush with death. Whenever death or some other serious physical threat comes near, the experience is invariably disturbing and disrupting. When the threat also involves evil and violence, the disturbance is greater still. Evil brings a certain unpredictability that has a disorientating effect all of its own.

It is particularly poignant that Tamar is violated by someone whom she might have looked to for help and protection. As her half-brother, Amnon could have been expected to help her flourish but instead he inflicted a violent assault and a demeaning humiliation. He "grabbed" Tamar and, although she resisted and pleaded with him, "he refused to listen to her and, since he was stronger than she, he raped her" (v 11, 14).

Power and powerlessness

Feeling unable to prevent or stop terrible things happening to us is a key element in the experience of trauma. Whether through unavoidable accident, natural disaster or malicious violence, an inability to avoid or escape harm is invariably present in trauma. Those who have experienced traumatic events often identify powerlessness and lack of agency as one of the most disturbing parts of the experience. Indeed, even people who are not being harmed can feel traumatised when they witness the suffering of others yet find themselves unable to do anything to help.

Tamar was powerless to resist the manipulation that put her in danger in the first place. King David commanded her to go to Amnon's house, and she had to obey. She was powerless before the men who wielded authority over her, and then, finally, she was physically powerless in the physical violence of the rape itself.

In the aftermath, her powerlessness continues. Despite her protestations, she is thrown out, and the door is barred behind her. Her brother, Absalom, finding her in distress and perceiving what has happened, begins to make decisions for her. She has no voice with Amnon and no voice with Absalom—one "refused to listen to her" and the other tells her to "be quiet" (v 14, 20). Is Absalom wanting to quieten her weeping or warning her not to speak of what has been done to her? In either case, from this point on, Tamar has no agency in the decision-making that follows.

We see another expression of the misuse of power in the actions, or more accurately the *in*actions, of her father, King David. It seems positive that "when David heard all this, he was furious" (v 21). But then we realise that the emotion is not followed by action. King David doesn't *do* anything. He has power: the power to bring justice, the power to condemn the guilty and the power to bring solace and care to the victim. He does none of these things.

Perhaps we should not be surprised. David's use of power has already been shown to be wanting, for he has used it, not in the pursuit of justice, but for his own selfish gains. His behaviour with Bathsheba has disturbing resonances with the sexual abuse demonstrated by Amnon (2 Samuel 11).

David, too, used power to take advantage of a woman sexually and was then guilty of cold-blooded violence in arranging the death of her husband, Uriah. Some attitudes, it seems, tumble down the generations.

Humiliation and disgrace

Not all trauma involves wrong being inflicted on another. But when it does, the sense of shame can be pronounced. This is especially true in the aftermath of sexual violence. In her appeal to Amnon, Tamar speaks of the disgrace she will endure because he has raped her (13:16). Victims of sexual abuse often describe feeling dirty or soiled because of what has happened to them. It can seem to them that they are tarnished or ruined. Many will also feel responsible for the assault, as if it was something that they did or failed to do which caused this to happen to them.

The biblical narrative doesn't report the feelings Tamar experienced in the aftermath of the assault. But it does tell us that she "put ashes on her head and tore the ornate robe she was wearing" and that, with her hands on her head, she "went away, weeping aloud as she went" (v 19). The ornate robe was "the kind of garment the virgin daughters of the king wore" (v 18). Tamar tearing that robe symbolises not just the loss of her virginity but the loss of status and dignity as well. The ashes on her head indicate a kind of abasement, expressing her sense of worthlessness. Putting her hands on her head intensifies the expression of all that she feels. She feels she must cover her shame and hide herself from everyone's gaze. Disgrace and desolation cling to her.

A Bible full of trauma

The account of Tamar's suffering is both shocking and brutal, but it is not the Bible's only account of severe suffering. Scripture describes many traumatic events: Hagar is driven into the wilderness with her child (Genesis 21)—a single mother abandoned and alone. Joseph is beaten, stripped and sold into slavery, falsely accused and unjustly imprisoned (Genesis 37 – 40).

The catalogue of suffering goes on and on. Jeremiah, Daniel and Job all endure terrible trials. The New Testament is also filled with traumatic events: the "murder of the innocents" on King Herod's orders in Matthew 2 may be recorded only briefly, but the agony is vividly captured in the prophetic words of Jeremiah that Matthew quotes:

> *"A voice is heard in Ramah,*
> *weeping and great mourning,*
> *Rachel weeping for her children*
> *and refusing to be comforted,*
> *because they are no more." (Matthew 2:18)*

Similarly, the stoning of Stephen in Acts 7 receives only a brief mention, but the brutality is clear. Those who kill him are "yelling", they "rushed at him" and "dragged him" and "began to stone him" (v 57-58). The slow death from stoning is awful to imagine. Which of his friends witnessed the scene, and what impact did it have on them?

Communal trauma

As well as these accounts of individual trauma, the Bible also contains many accounts of trauma affecting whole communities. There is slavery, oppression and forced labour (Exodus 1), as well as famine (Ruth 1) and drought (1 Kings 17). Jephthah's unnamed daughter suffers a terrible fate: the victim of her father's thoughtless vow—a vow that he will not retract. The trauma felt because of her death extends beyond her close family. Each year, her tragic fate is remembered by the young women of Israel (Judges 11:40).

Brutal wars (1 Kings 22) and merciless sieges (2 Kings 6) are all part of the unfolding biblical narrative. God's people are driven from their land (2 Kings 25) and forced into exile—strangers in a foreign land (Psalm 137). Appalling hardship and intense suffering fill the biblical narrative. Trauma isn't new.

In response to their suffering, God's people cry out. The laments in the Psalms frequently have as their backdrop traumatic events. "How long, LORD?" asks the psalmist (Psalm 13:1). "I am overwhelmed with troubles … your wrath has swept over me; your terrors have destroyed me" (Psalm 88:3, 16). In the book of Job, we find his agonised complaints expressing the bewilderment of a believer wrestling for faith in the face of suffering.

What is clear, even from this brief survey, is that the Bible never shies away from suffering and struggle. The dark realities of life and the terrible suffering people endure are never airbrushed out of the biblical account. Scripture faces these experiences head-on. What good news that is for us when we face this kind of suffering ourselves or want to walk alongside those who have done so.

Brutality and beauty

We can't speak of violent and traumatic events in the New Testament without speaking of the central event itself—the cross of Jesus Christ. His arrest and brutal flogging and the almost unimaginable horror of his crucifixion stand at the very heart of the Christian faith. Mary watched her son die such a death. All the traumas of the Bible climax here.

Yet, when the apostle John describes this shameful and brutal death, the word he chooses is glory. In dying, Jesus is "glorified". And John's choice of that word is not original to him. He takes it from his Master. "Father, the hour has come," Jesus says as he prays on the night of his arrest:

"Glorify your Son, that your Son may glorify you" (John 17:1).

Brutality is overtaken by beauty. Darkness is followed by light. Terrible, tragic loss becomes the source of glorious God-given grace. The gospel is the most extraordinary reversal. The story of the cross offers an ultimate transformation that can speak to any and every trauma.

In the pages that follow, as we try to bring a biblical perspective to contemporary experiences of trauma, we will find that we are well equipped. Scripture speaks to these experiences. The gospel has words of comfort and hope more powerful than any words we might muster up. We have something to say.

Yet in order to speak, we must first listen. Faithful comfort and loving hope are always best communicated by those who have taken time to fully understand the sufferings of another. Our first task, then, is to consider the way trauma is being defined and some of the ways that we will encounter it in the local church.

Questions for reflection

1. Why do you think suffering and struggle is given such prominence in Scripture?
2. Which aspects of the effect on Tamar of her suffering particularly struck you? Were there any you had not really considered before?
3. How does it affect you to remember that the climactic suffering in the Bible is the suffering of Jesus himself?

CHAPTER 2

WHAT *IS* TRAUMA?

Although the Bible never uses the language of "trauma" in the way we do today, it does, as we have seen, describe many traumatic experiences of suffering and their effects. The language we use to describe these experiences has changed over time. "Shell shock" was used during the First World War to describe a disturbance seen in some soldiers following the experience of trench warfare. This typically involved features like profound anxiety, amnesia, shaking, tics and other physical expressions of psychological distress. While initially met with a sympathetic response, this shell-shocked state soon came to be seen as weakness or even moral failing. Sufferers were expected to learn to face their struggle in a more "manly" way. It would be fair to say that hundreds of thousands of men who had fought in the war, on both sides, lived with and struggled with trauma, unacknowledged and therefore unassisted, for the rest of their lives—with the inevitable effects on their families.

Similar struggles emerged in the Second World War and during the war in Vietnam. The care and support of Vietnam veterans became a key driver for further research and study. One particular cluster of symptoms was identified and came to be given the label "post-traumatic stress disorder" (PTSD). This diagnosis, to which we will return, was first included in psychiatry's diagnostic manuals in 1980.

Much more recently, one book above all others has popularised the topic of trauma. Bessel Van der Kolk's best-seller

The Body Keeps the Score[1] is a detailed summary of scientific research studies and trauma theories set alongside a compendium of treatment approaches. Given this, its popularity is remarkable. The book has spent more than 245 weeks on the *New York Times* best-seller list, 35 of those at number 1. The concept of trauma is now very much part of the modern Western mindset.

But before we move any further, we need to specify what we actually mean when we speak of trauma.

Wounds and scars

Defining trauma is difficult.

The word is derived from the Latin "to wound". But the wounding being described when people talk about trauma varies widely. Doctors use trauma to describe severe medical injuries—so, for instance, in the UK, the National Health Service identifies Cambridge University Hospitals as a major trauma centre, by which it means that acute medical care is provided there for major traumatic injuries such as those suffered in serious road-traffic accidents.

In other contexts, however, the wounding that is being described by the word trauma focusses on the emotional response that is made to particular experiences that are extremely distressing. It *could* involve a physical injury but need not do so.

Another use of the word is to refer to the ongoing psychological state that exists as a result of some kind of prior stress. In this case, we might say that the wound has become something like a painful scar, which disturbs and disrupts functioning into the future.

Even within this third way of using the word "trauma",

---

1 *The Body Keeps the Score: Brain, Mind, and Body in the Healing of Trauma* (Penguin, 2015).

however, there is a variety of usages. Some would only describe a person as being traumatised in this ongoing sense if that person had experienced extreme suffering—for instance, some kind of terrible accident or sexual assault or being caught up in a warzone or a natural disaster. These are generally experiences in which life comes under threat. Some writers refer to this as "big-T" trauma.

This contrasts with "little-t" trauma, in which a person experienced something distressing and disturbing but which was not at the most severe end. Studies using these "little-t" definitions report finding that 70% of people have experienced trauma in their lives.[2] This makes exposure to trauma normal, and so attention switches to trying to understand why some people develop ongoing difficulties as a result of their experience and some do not.

Current confusion

Because the word "trauma" is used in all these different ways, misunderstandings are inevitable. When someone talks about trauma, they may be doing so in a colloquial and casual way or with a formal medical diagnosis in mind. It's somewhat similar to our use of the word "depression", which can also be used in a very wide range of different ways.

The Covid pandemic only increased references to trauma. Lockdown experiences were identified as a society-wide trauma that affected all of us. It was an opinion piece about our experience of lockdowns that spoke of "how trauma became the word of the decade".[3]

---

2 "Post Traumatic Stress Disorder stats and figures", https://www.ptsduk.org/ptsd-stats/ (accessed 19th August 2024).
3 Lexi Pandell, "How trauma became the word of the decade", vox.com/the-highlight/22876522/trauma-covid-word-origin-mental-health (accessed 29th May 2024).

The problem with the language of trauma becoming more and more widely used is that it begins to lose its meaning altogether. If everything negative is trauma, then in one sense it becomes a meaningless term. The focus of this book will be on "big T" trauma—on the rarer and more exceptional events (whether one-off or repeated) that result in people experiencing ongoing struggles in daily life.

In one sense, then, an understanding of trauma is straightforward. Someone experiences something terrible, and the experience is traumatising for them. We all face troubling events, but the severity of such events varies. It might be thought, therefore, that we could simply rank troubling events on a scale ranging from mild to severe and then identify as traumatic anything which involves an event lying beyond a certain threshold on the scale.

The reality, however, is far more complex. This is because different people respond to the same event in different ways. Past experience, cultural expectations and something identified as personal resilience all play a part in determining the impact a distressing event has upon an individual. (That said, some take issue with the idea of resilience because of the way it can be used to critique people: "Why can't you just be a bit more resilient?")

This is why there is no universally agreed definition of trauma. Here is a selection of some of the more common definitions used by different organisations:

"Trauma is an emotional response to a terrible event like an accident, crime, natural disaster, physical or emotional abuse, neglect, experiencing or witnessing violence, death of a loved one, war, and more."[4]

(American Psychological Association)

---

4 apa.org/topics/trauma/ (accessed 29th May 2024).

> *"Trauma refers to the way that some distressing events are so extreme or intense that they overwhelm a person's ability to cope, resulting in lasting negative impact."*[5]
> *(UK Trauma Council)*

> *"Psychological trauma is a person's experience of emotional distress resulting from an event that overwhelms the capacity to emotionally digest it."*[6]
> *(Psychology Today)*

> *"[Trauma is the result of] an event or repeated experience where the person felt terrified and powerless to defend themselves, and then [was] unable to process or make sense of the experience."*[7]
> *(Trauma Informed Churches)*

Finally, it is worth noting this definition from Darby Strickland:

> *"The word trauma refers to the emotional, spiritual, and physical disruptions that occur when a person is overwhelmed by extreme suffering."*[8]

Notice that two elements are prominent. The first is a distressing event outside the range of usual human experience (though quite what we should consider normal and what we should consider unusual then becomes the question). Often this event involves an encounter with death—a person may experience a direct threat of death themselves or it may involve the death of someone else, which they may or may not have directly witnessed.

The second element is an experience of helplessness or

---

5 uktraumacouncil.org/trauma/trauma (accessed 29th May 2024).
6 psychologytoday.com/gb/basics/trauma (accessed 7th August 2024).
7 traumainformedchurches.org/trauma-vs-mental-health (accessed 13th February 2024).
8 *Trauma: Caring for Survivors* (P&R, 2023), p. 3.

powerlessness. This experience of being unable to defend yourself from harm or being unable to escape from the threat of harm seems to be an important factor in making an event traumatic.

Three E's

One much quoted definition describes trauma as "an event or circumstance resulting in physical harm, emotional harm and/or life-threatening harm. The event or circumstance has lasting adverse effects on the individual's mental, physical and emotional health, as well as on social and/or spiritual well-being."[9] This definition captures what have been called the three E's of trauma:[10]

There is an *event* (or series of events)…

> … in which a person *experiences* themselves as powerless as they face something they can neither cope with nor process and…

> > … which then produces an ongoing *effect* on that person's functioning.

Event: As we've seen, the event could be an isolated incident, or it could be a repeated series of events extending over many years—for instance domestic abuse, long-term illness or repeated discrimination and bullying. Trauma caused by a protracted series of events has a more complicated impact on a person, and when those events occur during childhood, the distinct label of "complex trauma" is often used.[11]

---

9 samhsa.gov/trauma-violence (accessed 7th August 2024).

10 Substance Abuse and Mental Health Services Administration, "SAMHSA's Concept of Trauma and Guidance for a Trauma-Informed Approach" in HHS Publication No. (SMA) 14-4884 (Substance Abuse and Mental Health Services Administration, 2014), p. 8.

11 https://uktraumacouncil.org/trauma/complex-trauma (accessed 9th August 2024).

Experience: Many factors will affect the way an individual experiences what has happened to them. In a family which experiences a burglary, two siblings might both have been present in the house when it happened, but one child might find the burglary deeply traumatic while the other does not. Age can play a part, affecting both a child's awareness of the events and their capacity to comprehend them. Different interpretations may also be given to what has taken place. For instance, one child may consider themselves somehow responsible for what happened. They may carry this sense of responsibility into the future without anyone being aware of that.

Our experience of a traumatic event will also be affected by our pre-existing understanding of the world. What we have been led to expect or what we have seen happening in the world around us can profoundly affect our experience of an event because it affects the way we interpret events. That could be due to a Buddhist belief in karma or a Christian theology of suffering. Such a framework does not, of course, make a person impervious to trauma, but it impacts the experience.

Effects: Many definitions of trauma include mention of the way a person's life is impacted. Trauma can affect a person's functioning and wellbeing in a whole range of ways, both physical and spiritual. A person caught up in a house fire could be left with disfiguring burns. A victim of an assault might have a brain injury. A stress-related illness could be precipitated by or exacerbated by trauma. The frequency and severity of migraines, for example, might increase significantly following trauma. The development of addictive patterns of behaviour is not unusual either, to dampen the level of arousal a person is feeling or to distract from the presence of intrusive thoughts. Alcohol or drug addictions are common, and of course these have their own set of physical effects.

The spiritual and psychological impact of trauma can be expressed in many different ways. Relationships are commonly affected. Trust may have been undermined. Confidence may have been eroded as well as the capacity to manage social situations. Increased isolation might go hand in hand with difficulties in employment or caring for family. Mental-health struggles often include low mood and symptoms of anxiety. Thinking more specifically about Christian believers who experience trauma, some more obvious kinds of spiritual struggle would include finding it almost impossible to pray and equally impossible to meet with other believers, especially in the context of a main church gathering. A person's relationship with the Lord might well be disturbed as new doubts arise.

Post-traumatic stress disorder (PTSD)

The best-known impact of trauma is that described as PTSD. This is a psychiatric diagnosis that is given to a person when a series of specific features are present. The fifth version of the DSM (Diagnostic and Statistical Manual) includes the following features:

1. An exposure to actual or threatened death, serious injury, or sexual violence which can occur either through direct experience or through witnessing, (or in certain cases hearing about) the event happening to someone else.

2. Intrusive symptoms—such as distressing memories (often referred to as flashbacks) or disturbing dreams or nightmares. These intrusive symptoms may be associated with something called dissociation, which involves a variable degree of disconnection with the present.

3. Avoidance—this may involve avoiding situations or events which remind them of the original traumatic event.
4. Negative changes in cognition or mood—this might involve a person holding exaggerated negative beliefs about themselves or their thinking being dominated by self-blame. There may be a loss of interest in, or disengagement from, normal life activities and a persistent state of negative emotions like fear, anger or shame.
5. Hyper-arousal—expressed in irritability or anger, hyper-vigilance, difficulty in concentrating or sleep disturbance.

Other ways in which writers describe the impact of trauma include the impact on memory, the body and relationships. We will look at these in chapters 7-9.

An overwhelming experience

It is crucial to understand that the experience of extreme suffering can overwhelm someone. The inability to process what has happened in that suffering can impact them in a wide range of different ways and may have profound and long-lasting effects in their life.

A basic awareness of the way people can be affected by trauma will help us to avoid overlooking such struggles in those around us, or failing to consider that behaviour which seems strange or awkward to us may be due to the impact of trauma. A church that is unfamiliar with the way severe suffering can affect a person will fail to care well for such people in their congregation and community. So in the next chapter, we'll meet some traumatised people, and see how easy it is for a well-intentioned church to fail to understand and love them well.

Questions for reflection

1. Before you came to this chapter, how did you understand the use of the word "trauma"?
2. Why might it matter if we begin to use the word "trauma" casually to refer to minor difficulties?
3. What do you think churches need to know if they are going to engage well with someone who has been diagnosed with PTSD?

CHAPTER 3

ENCOUNTERING TRAUMA

Since trauma will sometimes be a significant factor in pastoral care, it is important to be alert to it. Yet trauma is often hidden—in fact, at times it may even be hidden from the person themselves. When we fail to see the way an experience of trauma is contributing to a pastoral situation, we risk significant pastoral missteps.

The examples that follow describe just some of the many ways trauma might affect people in our churches. Each illustration begins with a pastoral encounter that was puzzling or problematic. What follows is the backstory which helps explain why that initial pastoral contact happened in the way it did.

None of the stories describe real individuals but are composite stories reflecting the experiences of many different people that I have known. I have chosen not to include an account of someone who had experienced childhood trauma. This is not because this kind of trauma is either rare or unimportant. Rather, it is because I was conscious that, in a short account, I might struggle to do justice to the complexity of such experiences or of the far-reaching impact they can have on a person's life. In my suggestions for further reading, I have included a book by Mez McConnell, which describes his experience of "finding faith in God through childhood abuse".

The first two illustrations are longer and give a fuller picture of the impact that trauma can have upon a person. The remainder are briefer outlines intended to help indicate the broad range of ways we might encounter trauma in pastoral settings.

Morten and his home group

Ben and Niko had just started leading a small group in their church. It was their first experience of this kind of leadership. After only a month, they were already beginning to have concerns about a man called Morten who was new to the church. He had failed to turn up to the first meeting, and although he contacted them the next day to apologise, the same thing happened the following week. When they saw him on Sunday at church, Morten explained that he was struggling a bit at the moment and wondered if a daytime group might be better for him. His reasoning didn't make much sense to them, and when they pressed for more detail, he seemed a bit evasive.

After missing a third meeting, he explained that he was feeling anxious about coming out at night. This seemed strange since they knew that he had previously been serving as part of the Street Pastors team in their town, which had meant routinely being out into the small hours. Nevertheless, they decided they probably ought to offer some kind of help. So they suggested that if it was necessary, they could see about arranging for someone to call round and walk with Morten to the home group. When Morten said he didn't want that, it seemed to Ben and Niko that they had done what they could and that Morten wasn't really co-operating. They told Morten to get back in touch if he changed his mind. Several months passed, and no further contact came.

Morten's story

A couple of years earlier, Morten had been mugged. It happened after a meal out with friends. He was on his way back to the bus stop when a moped mounted the pavement, and before he knew what was happening, someone had his shoulder bag in their grasp. He clung to the bag out of instinct, but as the moped raced past, the bag was ripped from his hands. All that his attempts to hang on to the bag achieved was to pull him violently to the ground. His head hit the pavement, and he blacked out. He had a broken nose, a fractured cheekbone and also a dislocated shoulder. When he came round, there was blood coming from his nose and lots of blood from a deep gash on his head. It still isn't entirely clear how long he was unconscious. It was a quiet street which had been deserted at the time of the assault. At first he was unable even to pull himself up to sitting. So he just lay still, frightened and in pain.

He remembers that lasting for ages—lying there utterly alone and wondering how badly he was injured. Eventually someone came down the street, found Morten on the ground and called the emergency services. It is the experience of lying alone—still hazy in his mind—that is the worst part of his ordeal.

The police were sympathetic, but no arrests were made and Morten's belongings were never recovered. Memories of his time in hospital are vague, but he does recall just how painful the treatments for his broken nose and dislocated shoulder were.

Two years on, the events still replay in his mind. Feelings of panic can suddenly rise—typically late at night. Often it is as if he is back on the pavement, in pain and alone. It's hard to shake himself out of those memories—they are so vivid. Sometimes it doesn't pass until he gets out of bed and goes downstairs to make himself some tea. Traffic noises, especially the sound of motor bikes or mopeds, are enough to stir intense anxiety. He tries to avoid being out near traffic of any kind, especially at night.

Before the assault Morten had been regular at his church home group, active in church life and a regular volunteer in the local Street Pastors scheme. But in the immediate aftermath of the mugging, he barely went out at all. The mugging had happened close to the building where his church met, and on the first Sunday when he tried to get back to church, it stirred such horrible and vivid memories of what had happened that he retraced his steps and returned home. The same thing happened the following Sunday, and for more than a year he didn't get to church at all. The leadership were understanding at first, but gradually they stopped being in touch.

Eighteen months later, he decided to try a church in a different part of town so that he wouldn't need to go near the place where the mugging had happened. He asked to join a small group and was allocated to a group led by a friendly couple called Ben and Niko. They lived local to his home, and he felt sure that would make it easy to get along. But the anxiety was overwhelming and getting there proved too difficult.

He tried to tell Ben and Niko about his worries, but it all seemed so silly, and he couldn't quite find the words. He felt ashamed that he couldn't just trust God and make the 15-minute walk to their house. Part of him felt foolish and too embarrassed to explain his fears. Yet at other times, the intensity of those fears left him feeling completely paralysed.

When Ben and Niko offered to come and get him, it only made him feel more foolish. And perhaps it was just his imagination, but Morten had the impression that everyone in the home group thought it faintly ridiculous that he couldn't get there on his own. How could he expect them to understand the strength of his experiences? He decided it was easier simply to withdraw from the group altogether. That was nine months ago, and the leaders haven't really stayed in touch.

Naomi and her email

The email that arrived in the church office was distinctly unusual. Aisha, who worked there part-time, read it twice but still couldn't quite make sense of it. It seemed so odd that she wondered if she should simply delete it. But eventually she decided to mention it to the pastor. The email was asking about arranging a meeting with someone from the church but gave no details about why a meeting was wanted or what the meeting would be about. The person writing also said they would like to choose who they met with and asked if they could have a list of options. What seemed to Aisha as particularly odd was that the email stipulated that the meeting had to take place away from the church building. It was all so very demanding, and it really didn't help that the tone of the email was so abrupt. The pastor checked the name of the sender but didn't recognise it. He said it was definitely odd and that he'd think about it before replying. That had been more than a week ago. Aisha suspected he had probably forgotten. She couldn't decide whether to remind him or simply to delete the email and forget it.

Naomi's story

The email was from Naomi. She struggles even to enter a church building. For Naomi, church buildings are just too deeply associated with what happened to her.

Ten years ago, as a new believer, she was just beginning to get to know the church she had joined. She was both impressed by and grateful for the attention that the pastor was giving her. He seemed so understanding of the questions she had about her new faith. The time he took to listen to her and answering her questions was proving so very helpful.

Looking back, she still can't quite see what she missed. Nothing in his manner in those early days alerted her to what lay ahead. It all happened so gradually. At first his strong encouragements to make time for church meetings and to join him for one-to-one Bible studies seemed a wonderfully generous gift of his time. She felt prized and appreciated—and this was in stark contrast to the way men usually treated her. Almost every male friend she'd ever had seemed to have taken advantage of her. Disillusionment with those relationships had, in fact, been one of the driving forces for exploring the Christian faith in the first place. Jesus seemed so different. When she read the Gospel accounts, she loved the way Jesus treated women.

At first the pastor seemed just like that: patient, gentle, attentive—he really seemed to care, and he took time to listen to her. No one had done that before. When he hugged her as she left his house, she so appreciated it. It added to her sense that she was special and that he really cared about her. Visits to his home became frequent. Usually there was some Bible study and then practical tasks that he needed help with. There always seemed to be a church event that needed preparing for, and she liked to feel useful.

Quite when or how those hugs moved from friendly embraces to something rather different Naomi still can't quite say. It happened so gradually that the alarm bells never sounded. Only looking back can she see how he was testing the water as he gradually became more physical with her.

He used Scripture to justify the sexual relationship that developed. He was so persuasive, and, of course, he knew the Bible in a way that she didn't. He told her that their relationship served God—that it was important for his ministry and was helping him to fulfil his calling. He emphasised that their relationship must be kept secret. Others, he said, would misinterpret what was happening. They wouldn't understand how God was using her to support the spread of the gospel through him. Things settled into a pattern, and she remembers feeling increasingly trapped. But if she did express concerns, he just confused her with clever words that left her feeling under tremendous pressure to continue.

Then, gradually, his kindness gave way to a more demanding and controlling attitude towards her. He wanted to know who she was seeing and how she was using her free time. He made demands about the way she dressed and how much she saw of her family. She can't remember exactly when it was that his harshness finally moved into physical violence, but she does remember how frightened she became. She dreaded what he might do if she tried to bring their relationship to an end.

She is ashamed, looking back, that it took so long before she finally confided in someone else. She did once mention to others in the church some general concerns about their pastor, but they defended him so strongly that she was convinced no one would ever believe her if she told them what was actually going on. It was a visit to her GP that eventually brought things to a head. Her GP suspected she had a sexually transmitted disease and asked her about her sexual activity. That's when it all came out, and before she knew it, she was swept up into a nightmarish safeguarding process.

Though that did bring their relationship to a close, it didn't really end things. The impact of what he had done clung to her. She felt used. She kept remembering verses from the Bible which he had quoted to persuade her to do things she had never wanted to do. Everything about the Christian faith now felt bound up with his manipulation and control. The strange thing is that, despite it all, she still believed. Her faith remained intact—but she couldn't seem to find a way to engage with God without the experience of his abuse filling her head.

The safeguarding process took for ever. Going back over everything wasn't easy. It often felt as if that process was mostly about the church authorities ticking all the right boxes. The impact that he had had upon her and the impact that the safeguarding process was now having on her didn't seem to be anyone's priority. In a strange way, she felt used and controlled in that process too.

She moved away as soon as she could. Some months later, she felt drawn to try and engage with church again. Despite what had happened, she still wanted to be part of a faith community. Only she couldn't get through the door. The first Sunday she tried, feelings of panic began to build when just walking toward the church. When the church building actually came into sight, she felt physically sick. She just turned and walked away. It was much the same at home when she tried to open the Bible—it just seemed to remind her of the way that Bible verses had been used to control her. She had never felt so ashamed and so stuck.

And that is why she decided to send an email to the church office. She wanted to see if she could meet with someone—preferably a woman—but she knew the meeting would have to happen away from the church building. She tried to explain what she wanted, but the words were so hard to write. Still, she managed to get something typed and sent. But Naomi is worried they will just think she's being difficult and ignore her. It's been over a week now, and she still hasn't had a reply.

Anna's story

Anna was asked to help in crèche. Although she initially seemed keen and agreed to join the rota, after only one Sunday helping in crèche she contacted the organiser and asked to pull out. When asked why, she seemed reticent to explain more and simply said it wasn't for her.

Some years previously, Anna had witnessed the death of her sister's child. She was visiting the family when the toddler became unwell. A high fever was quickly followed by the appearance of an angry rash. The toddler was distressed at first, but within hours he became stiller and quieter and couldn't be persuaded to drink anything. While Anna sat with the child, the parents tried to seek medical support. But in what seemed like only a matter of minutes, her nephew deteriorated further, and Anna realised he had stopped breathing. While they waited for the ambulance, the emergency operator tried to describe how they could provide resuscitation. When the paramedics arrived, they took over, but despite their efforts and continued treatment at the emergency department, the child still died.

Anna has never really spoken about this experience. At some level, she blames herself for what happened. The thought that a child in crèche could become unwell and that she would be responsible for that as well feels just too much to bear.

Bandhu's story

Bandhu hovers on the edge of church. He often seems distant and disengaged. Despite encouragements he never wants to join any of the midweek activities. To many, he seems depressed.

Bandhu's best friend at university took his own life just before second-year exams. Bandhu still can't make sense of it. He had seen him on the morning of the day he died and is still plagued with the thought that he should have noticed something. He wonders whether, if he had, his friend might still be alive. Bandhu still has vivid memories of what his friend looked like when he found him dead in his room.

Craig's story

Craig is a volunteer leader with his church's youth group. The overall leader has arranged a weekend away and wants Craig to look after the music. But much to the overall leader's annoyance, Craig refuses point blank and says that he isn't willing to come on the weekend at all.

Some years ago, Craig was involved in a multiple-vehicle car crash. It happened on the motorway in dense fog. Although he himself was unhurt, people in the car alongside him died. He recalls the noise of the accident and people's cries and that awful wait for the arrival of the emergency services. The whole thing is etched in his mind like some kind of awful tableau full of disturbing images. The ongoing effects are strange—for example, Craig never used to look at porn, but that has become a habit since the accident. In the short term, it both distracts him and provides a kind of comfort. But the relief is brief, and the shame and guilt last much longer.

As for the youth weekend, Craig knows the only way to travel to there will be by car. And Craig avoids car journeys whenever he can—especially on motorways.

Erica's story

Erica is demanding. Her many complaints leave people exhausted, as do her constant requests for help and support with her children. Though they don't really admit it to themselves, many people in church now do all they can to avoid her altogether. Those that persist with her have usually found some way of managing her incessant demands.

Erica was in an abusive marriage for more than a decade. The mix of emotional manipulation, controlling behaviour and occasional physical violence took its toll. Over the years, she has been told so many times that she is nothing more than a useless waste of space. Now she struggles to see herself in any other terms. Threats of violence were used to intimidate and control her. Her sense of helplessness is profound. Sometimes it seems as if the only means she has of interacting with others is through the language of need.

Faheem's story

Faheem has been causing problems with the family who kindly offered to house him after he arrived in the country. He plays loud music at unsociable hours and seems unwilling or unable to interact in even the most basic ways with his host family. His hosts think it may be best if he moves somewhere else.

Faheem lived through the horrors of war and then as a refugee. The uncertainty of that period was profound. Day after day, he never knew when an attack would come or whether there would be food for him to eat. His helplessness as he hid from enemy troops still haunts him. While only a teenager, he was forced to watch the brutal killing of his own parents. No one knows about that—he worries that if he tells anyone, they won't believe him. The flashbacks are worst at night, and sometimes only music seems to be able to drown out the sounds and visions that fill his mind.

Graham's story

Although he had accepted an invitation to the church's welcome supper, Graham never came. When the church pastor followed up with Graham and sent a time for them to meet up and chat about church, he never replied. They had noticed that Graham was nervous when he arrived at church that first Sunday, but they also noticed that he was familiar with the songs and other aspects of the service. Graham had seemed much more at home in the weeks running up to the welcome supper, so it surprised them when he didn't come. And now he has disappeared completely and stopped answering emails as well.

Graham attended his previous church for 20 years. He was always eager to serve and over time came to work closely with the senior pastor. Looking back, he still can't work out when it was that the pastor began to take advantage of him.

The extent of what was expected from him slowly grew, and then so did the blunt emails that piled on the pressure and increased the demands. Soon there were phone calls that were polite and angry at the same time. They came whenever he failed to get things done exactly right. Graham came to dread opening his laptop for fear that another demanding email would be waiting for him. It affected his sleep, his mood, his work and his health. At times only alcohol numbed the intensity of the stress he was feeling. If it hadn't been for a junior staff member finally complaining to the church authorities, he wonders if he would have survived. When it was identified as extreme bullying and the range of people affected became clear, there was relief, but there was also a profound sense of shame. The fear of being treated badly by those in authority was so strong that it took him five years before he could even consider engaging with a church again.

Trauma comes in so many different forms and is so often hidden from view. Those around us in church may have stories of trauma about which we know nothing. Sometimes those stories will burst into the present in dramatic and disturbing ways; more often they will lurk in the background. But all the time, relationships are strained or impaired; daily functioning is disrupted; faith is challenged.

If we are going to support people who are carrying trauma, the most basic requirement is that we are alert to the category in the first place. Unless we consider that trauma is a possibility, we will invariably miss it. And if we miss it, we will never be able to speak the comfort of Christ into its midst.

But thoughts about how we might be able to offer help are still a long way off. First, we need to recognise how churches, instead of offering comfort for trauma, can sometimes contribute to it.

Questions for reflection

1. Which of these stories do you find most disturbing, and why?

2. Why do you think traumatic experiences so often remain hidden?

3. In many of the stories set out in this chapter, people jumped to false conclusions about why people were behaving as they were. What can help us to avoid doing that?

CHAPTER 4

TRAUMA AND CHURCH

Because the language of trauma is being used much more widely today than it once was, both those hearing the gospel for the first time and those who have been in church for decades are increasingly aware of the category. If our churches, and particularly our pastors, know little about trauma—or simply misunderstand it—we are at risk of speaking unhelpfully. At best we may sound clumsy and out of touch; at worst our words will prove alienating and hurtful. If we are going to commend Christ well in contemporary culture, we need to understand the issues that our contemporary culture considers important. And that includes trauma.

Engaging well with trauma, though, involves much more than simply improving our communication. Understanding the way trauma impacts individuals should also inform the way we organise our ministry and our activities. We want to be alert to anyone whose experience of trauma has left them in some sense vulnerable to further harm. This isn't simply about protecting the reputation of the church; it is about caring well and not inflicting harm. Churches who minister the gospel will want to do these things as well as they can. The New Testament consistently appeals to churches to demonstrate such compassion (for instance, Ephesians 4:32; Philippians 2:1-2; Colossians 3:12; 1 Peter 3:8).

This chapter aims to help churches avoid causing hurt or damage. Sometimes that can come about simply through missteps—the kind that happen either through ignorance or simply failing to think things through. At other times, however, the pain a church inflicts comes not because of a misstep but sadly as the result of ministry practices that are directly abusive. In recent years, many helpful books have outlined some of the ways that abuse can happen in the context of the church. A list is provided in the section on further reading. This chapter only offers a brief overview in this area. We will look first at harm that arises from ignorance, and then at that which comes from thoughtlessness before turning, finally, to harm that arises from abuse.

Church and harm

1. Harm from clumsiness because of ignorance
Whether we view the current level of interest in trauma in wider society positively or negatively, it should still affect the ministry we do.

In setting out qualifications for elders, Paul mentions the need for "a good reputation with outsiders" (1 Timothy 3:7). Paul is not, of course, advising compromise on the content of the gospel. The Christian gospel can often cause offence, and we must be ready for that. The bad reputation that Paul has in mind here is the avoidable kind—the kind that might arise out of moral lapses which would lead to a poor reputation, but also the kind that can arises out of clumsy words spoken through ignorance. If we don't understand the issues people feel strongly about, we can seem insensitive and out of touch. Simply recognising those issues is, however, not enough. Unless we have a proper understanding of them, we still risk misstepping by speaking clumsily out of ignorance.

Our contemporary culture expects those who care to have a basic awareness of the impact of trauma. Pastors who pay little attention to the category of trauma or are ignorant of the way trauma can affect people will therefore seem uncaring. Much more important than that, however, is that ignorance may lead us into doing actual harm to those whose past includes profound suffering.

Take, for example, someone who has been involved in military action and has witnessed appalling brutality. A sermon from 2 Kings 25 that deals with the account of Zedekiah's torture in a witty, light-hearted way will be mistaken in so many ways but will land particularly badly with a military veteran. Or think of a sermon from the passage with which we opened this book—the rape of Tamar in 2 Samuel 13—in which a preacher launches abruptly into the narrative without any apparent awareness of its potential impact on people who have experienced sexual violence. That not only risks looking thoughtless and foolish but may also cause significant harm. The same thoughtlessness can, of course, happen in the context of a small-group Bible study.

2. Harm from incompetence because of limited knowledge

A different kind of harm can arise when those offering pastoral support lack the skill to care well for someone who has experienced profound suffering. Those who work regularly with people who have experienced trauma follow a well-established process, which begins by establishing a context of safety and security. People need to be in a situation where they feel safe and which will keep them safe before they are invited to explore an experience of trauma from their past.

Someone unaware of this basic element of care risks making some fundamental errors. Suppose, for example, they have some vague notion about it being good to "get things off your chest". Or that someone who has had profound suffering needs to "come to terms with the past". With that limited rationale, they might encourage someone to talk through what has happened to them. However, doing that in a context where safety has not been established can be damaging. Experts refer to this as a kind of "retraumatisation".

There are many ways a church can press people into saying more than they want to. They may be urged to set out their need for healing or to list things for which they need to forgive others. They could be told that it is important to share with those in pastoral leadership because openness helps build church community.

Remembering traumatic events has a distinctive quality. It often causes a person not just to recall things as something from the past but to re-experience them in the present. The same emotions are felt in the present just as they were felt in the original suffering. Remember, also, that trauma is associated with an experience of powerlessness. When someone is encouraged to recall a traumatic experience in a context where they feel unable to refuse, or where no one knows what to do when they become distressed, feelings of powerless may be prominent all over again. Once more, things feel out of control. Once more, no one is there to keep them safe. Revisiting past traumatic events involves this kind of re-experiencing and may include such a collapse of the sense of time that it can seem to a person as if they are back in the traumatic episode all over again. Hence the language of retraumatisation.

3. Harm from abuse because of malicious intent

Recent years have brought to light many kinds of abusive practice in a whole range of different churches. Some have involved sexual abuse of children or vulnerable adults. In other settings controlling and coercive forms of ministry have been identified. Those in positions of power have used their authority to satisfy their own interests at the expense of others. Diane Langberg has described such practices using references to Jesus' powerful imagery of a wolf in sheep's clothing (Matthew 7:15-16).[12] These are pastors who prey on the very flock they are supposed to be guarding and protecting. Instead of serving people entrusted to their care, they have served their own desires—whether narcissistic or sexual or both.

The impact of this kind of abuse obviously varies. It will depend on the extent of the abusive practices and the degree to which any given individual is caught up in them. But when a church leader uses their position of spiritual authority to control others, the experience of powerlessness can be profound. Coercive practices are supported by claims of divine authority and leveraged with suggestions of divine disapproval if the pastor's suggestions or preferences aren't followed, or even with threats of eternal consequences. The cumulative sense of fear and dread and the associated experiences of guilt and shame can be intensely traumatising.

Because this kind of trauma is specifically associated with a church, it will frequently affect a person's future involvement with a church community. When safety has been dramatically absent in a person's experience of church, trust is deeply damaged. Trusting a church again—or, more specifically, trusting a church leader—can be incredibly difficult. Entering a church building, opening a Bible or attending a pastoral meeting are all activities that are now associated with memories of abuse and trauma. Returning to those elements, or indeed any elements, of church life can seem utterly unimaginable.

Even when a person does find the courage to return to a church, they will do so with hesitation and are likely to maintain their distance. Someone might always arrive late

---

12 *Redeeming Power: Understanding Authority and Abuse in the Church* (Brazos Press, 2020), p. 139.

and leave early. They might only ever be willing to sit at the back and decline invitations to engage in conversation or other church events. They may avoid eye contact and only give brief answers. This may be interpreted as a kind of social or spiritual coldness, and others may respond accordingly. Integration into church is badly affected. It will proceed slowly, if at all. The effort may be abandoned prematurely on either side. For the person who has experienced abuse, instead of lessening their negative associations with church, these failed attempts to return to church only serve to reinforce them.

The experience of traumatic treatment from pastors is not the only way trauma can happen in the context of church. Sometimes it is pastors who are traumatised and members of the congregation who are guilty of abuse. Unreasonable demands exerted through bullying practices can be deeply damaging.

The dynamics of power relationships in church are complicated, and we should avoid simplistic formulations. All of us have some measure of power, and each of us is responsible for using that power in ways which are pleasing to God. The pattern of servant leadership set for us by Christ has implications in every sphere of life and radically subverts our understanding of power in human relationships. We are all slow learners in this regard.

James warns teachers and, by implication, all those in authority that they will be judged more strictly (James 3:1). Jesus reserves some of his sternest critiques for the spiritual leaders of his day, who "tie up heavy, cumbersome loads and put them on other people's shoulders, but they themselves are not willing to lift a finger to move them" (Matthew 23:4). Yet every Christian disciple is called to walk in the footsteps of the one who "made himself nothing by taking the very nature of a servant" (Philippians 2:7): the one who "did not come to be served, but to serve" and lay down his life for others (Mark 10:45).

A basic expectation of any Christian church is that it will not cause harm to others. This obviously means identifying and eradicating every form of abuse in our churches. But it also means identifying the ways in which we, as our church, can cause harm inadvertently by a failure to care well for those who have experienced trauma in the past. To care well, we need to grow in our knowledge and understanding of the category of trauma, and to that we now turn.

Church and understanding

We need not think that every church must have in their midst experts in trauma studies and trauma recovery. What we should ask of ourselves is that we have the kind of understanding that will help our church communities to respond more wisely when we face pastoral issues associated with trauma.

Three things will contribute to this. First, a basic familiarity with the language and terms which are used in relation to trauma. It's hard to speak well with others when we don't know the language that is being used. Second, an awareness of the physiological mechanisms that are being identified as underpinning the experience of trauma. Our culture has become very familiar with the idea that "the body keeps the score". Applying the gospel faithfully will be easier when we understand the prominent ideas in our culture. Third, all those who care would benefit from having a broad outline of the main types of support that people affected by trauma are usually offered. A familiarity with this secular support will help churches and pastors understand the kind of input people are likely to be receiving, and it will also help them to make gospel connections with that help.

Of course, in each church there will be varying degrees of familiarity with the area of trauma and its treatment. Your church may well include some who work in the caring professions and engage with trauma in their day-to-day work, or whose secular training has prompted a particular interest in trauma studies. Such secular training and experience needs to be considered within a biblical worldview and the extent to which people will have done this will vary.

Others will have had a personal experience of trauma or will have seen its impact in the lives of those close to them. People who have this direct or indirect experience are sometimes passionate in their desire to raise awareness about trauma. This can make them valuable champions regarding church involvement. Less helpfully it can, sometimes, lead them to generalise their own experience and apply it to everyone else, preventing awareness of the many different ways in which trauma can affect a person, and of the fact that some people are not left traumatised by a significant adverse event.

Depending on their gifts and spiritual maturity, and their consideration of trauma from a Christian perspective, these people may be able to help with pastoral care and education. We may be able to tap into their knowledge, and they may be willing to play a part in helping to educate the church. It might be appropriate to encourage some in this group to develop their understanding further so that they can be even more helpful. This could be done either by additional secular training or by engaging with specifically Christian thinking in this area.

A second group in our churches—and probably the largest group—are those who are broadly aware of the topic of trauma but who lack any detailed knowledge. They have read and heard about trauma in the media and have the broadest sense of what is meant by the term but know their understanding is limited. Such people are often open to learning more not least because they are eager to be helpful to those impacted by trauma. Since you are reading this book, you may well be in this group. Thank you for reading!

A final group worthy of mention are those who take a sceptical and dismissive attitude toward trauma. This may arise because of a resistance to any perspectives arising from "the world's thinking". It can also be reinforced when the language of trauma is unhelpfully applied to more ordinary everyday trials and struggles. The challenge is to help those who are sceptical to see that the inappropriate application of these categories does not invalidate the very real impact of trauma in the experience of those who have faced life-altering events.

How a church might decide to grow in its understanding in this area will depend on many factors. The size of the church and the number in the church affected by trauma, as well as the church's existing familiarity with this issue, will all affect what might be most appropriate. But all of our churches can aim to develop sufficient awareness of the impact of trauma that we can respond thoughtfully, biblically and helpfully to those who carry these struggles from the past.

Church and care

Most churches will not feel they have the resources or the personnel available which allows them to offer skilled support to those who have suffered trauma. Occasionally a church will develop experience and skill in this area, or decide to develop a pastoral service with a specific focus on those who have experienced trauma. There might be a local Christian counselling service which can bring biblical expertise to bear.

More usually, and especially in smaller and medium-sized churches, such specialist provision will not be available. Yet we can still have a level of familiarity with trauma that enables us to walk alongside those who are getting skilled help elsewhere. This will mean a basic familiarity with the impact of trauma and with the kind of recovery paths people typically follow.

Signposting people to suitable care, and then supporting them as they receive that care, is a minimum target. It will also be helpful if churches provide a biblical framework that can sit alongside the secular care people are likely to be receiving. Knowing how to think biblically about suffering—including even extreme suffering—is an essential requirement. Knowing how to listen well, and how to stay involved with someone even when their emotional responses are both strong and complex, will also be key.

We might also helpfully recognise the differences between complex trauma (which arises from traumatic events experienced over a long period of time and especially in childhood) and single-event trauma. Complex trauma generally has a more extensive impact on relationships and a sense of safety which typically creates real complexities in all sorts of contexts, including in a person's relationship with helpers.

One aspect of care that church can and should always seek to excel in is perseverance. The Scriptures repeatedly emphasise the steadfast love of God. "The LORD, the LORD, a God merciful and gracious, slow to anger, and abounding in steadfast love and faithfulness" (Exodus 34:6, ESV). "Your steadfast love is great to the heavens, your faithfulness to the clouds" (Psalm 57:10, ESV). In imitation of the faithfulness of God, our churches should be steadfast in the support we offer those who have experienced extreme suffering. Our God is not quick to give up on us—no, he is patient beyond measure. "The LORD is good and his love endures for ever; his faithfulness continues through all generations" (Psalm 100:5). To imitate his faithfulness will mean continuing to support people even when little seems to be changing. It may also mean standing with people even when things just seem to be getting worse. It is not unusual to find that as a person begins to address trauma from the past, things get worse before they begin to get better. To imitate God's love will mean continuing to serve people even when we receive little or nothing in return.

So while not every Christian can or will become an expert, we can aim to have a sufficiently clear understanding of trauma that we can avoid causing harm. We will also want a knowledge of trauma that helps us to persevere. But our ambitions should go further. We should want a good enough understanding of trauma to enable us to speak well in this area of church life. We should be able to speak in such a way that not only do our churches avoid alienating those with experiences of trauma but we know how to hold out words of hope and life which will bring genuine encouragement in Christ.

Walking alongside those who have experienced trauma is hard. People who offer such support are undertaking a wonderful but also a wearying labour of love. They may need to be liberated from the pressure of always having to be there or of always knowing what to say. We must all be alert to the need to care for the carers so that their care can be sustained over the long term, which is so important in relation to recovery from trauma. And if you are the one who is walking alongside, you need to give yourself permission to find it hard, and to allow the wider church to help you.

Questions for reflection

1. How would you characterise the current level of understanding in your church in relation to trauma?
2. Of the various ways in which a church community might prove unsupportive to those who have experienced trauma, which might your church be most prone to?
3. What steps would help your church to become more familiar with the effects of trauma and more caring towards those who have experienced severe suffering?

CHAPTER 5

JESUS AND TRAUMA

In the next section, we will explore how recent studies describe the experience of trauma, and then in Section 3 we will consider how Christians can offer wise care to those who have suffered in this way. This chapter serves both as a backdrop and a preview, and we will think about its themes in more detail in later chapters. But we need to be clear early on: the life and ministry of Jesus Christ speaks to the issue of trauma. One of the great distinctives of the Christian faith is its focus on a Saviour who suffered. The redemption declared by the Christian faith comes to us only through the brutal—and traumatic—death of its founder. Christians should anticipate, therefore, that we will have a distinctive contribution to make to the understanding and care of those affected by trauma.

Jesus understands trauma

Luke chapter 8 is one of many chapters in the Gospel accounts where we see Jesus engaging with extreme suffering. Verses 22-25 describe a storm so severe that the disciples (despite some being experienced fishermen) are convinced that they are about to die. That is certainly a traumatic experience, yet one that we so easily skip over. Verses 26-39 concern a man so disturbed that the people of his town have chosen to put him in chains—yet he has broken those restraints. When Jesus encounters him, he is a desperate, naked man living a solitary life among the tombs. We can only guess at the kind of trauma that had marked his own life, as well as the lives of those closest to him.

The final section of the chapter (v 40-56) records two intertwined accounts. The first relates the story of a synagogue leader who is desperate because his 12-year-old daughter is close to death and he is powerless to help her. Sandwiched between the two halves of that story is another tale of woe. A woman approaches Jesus who has been "subject to bleeding for twelve years" and whom no one can heal (v 43). She was not only physically unwell but also, as was normal in 1st-century Jewish society, ostracised because of ritual uncleanness.

In a few short paragraphs, then, Luke has recorded four situations involving a whole range of different kinds of suffering. In each of them, death has come near: in two the threat is of imminent physical death, and the other two describe a kind of lingering death—years of suffering which have pushed the person, alone and helpless, to the very margins of their community.

Powerlessness is prominent in all these episodes. Some of the troubles are immediate and others longstanding; some involve illness and others are the result of what might be called natural disasters. All have left a deep impression on those involved, and all could have caused trauma to those involved. Whether they did prove traumatising will, as we've seen, have depended on many factors because trauma concerns Event, Experience *and* Effect. What is beyond doubt, however, is that in his incarnation, Jesus entered a world full of suffering. Jesus is no closeted religious leader or distant deity but one who came to the very front line of suffering. The difficult realities of trauma were all around him.

It wasn't just that Jesus understood suffering; it was also that he moved towards it, and did so with compassion. In a famous essay, the theologian B.B. Warfield noted that the most common emotion ascribed to Jesus is that of compassion (see, for instance, Luke 7:13, ESV).[13] Jesus is moved by need. In Luke 8 he responds to Jairus by going with him to his daughter. En route he is delayed by meeting the woman with the bleeding—having healed her, his words to her are "Go in peace" (v 48). Then, in response to the desperate news of the death of Jairus' daughter, Jesus tells him, "Don't be afraid; just believe, and she will be healed" (v 50). Jesus understood suffering and moved towards it.

Yet we can say more: Jesus didn't just see and move towards those burdened by extreme suffering and trauma; he experienced it himself.

Jesus experienced trauma

As in all of the four Gospel accounts, the climactic events in Luke's Gospel concern the arrest, trial and execution of Jesus Christ. The narrative is remarkably understated. As he relates the events, Luke gives little or no elaboration of the emotional impact upon Jesus. We learn more about the experience of those around Jesus than we do about Jesus himself. After he betrayed Jesus, Peter broke down and wept bitterly (Luke 22:62), and "a large number of people followed [Jesus to the cross], including women who mourned and wailed for him" (23:27). Yet we do see Jesus "in anguish" as the hour of his arrest came close—so emotionally stricken that "his sweat was like drops of blood falling to the ground" (22:44).

That Jesus experienced traumatic events is beyond doubt. He was arrested and mocked—exposed to shameful, public humiliation (23:11). The flogging he received was often enough to kill. And crucifixion has been described as the

---

13 "The Emotional Life of our Lord," monergism.com/thethreshold/sdg/warfield/TheEmotionalLifeofOurLord%20BBWarfield.pdf (accessed 7th August 2024), p. 6.

most barbaric form of execution ever inflicted. The physical pain from nailed hands and feet was endured under public gaze and lasted for many hours.

But for all the awfulness of the physical agonies, this wasn't the only or worst suffering that Jesus was facing on the cross. The Bible reveals a further experience of appalling suffering, for in his death, Jesus suffered hell—the spiritual judgment of his Father. "Christ redeemed us from the curse of the law by becoming a curse for us" (Galatians 3:13). As the pastor John Stott put it,

> "*The darkness of the sky was an outward symbol of the spiritual darkness which enveloped him ... 'outer darkness' was one of the expressions Jesus used for hell, since it is an absolute exclusion from the light of God's presence. Into that outer darkness the Son of God plunged for us.*"[14]

A crucified person, pinned to a wooden cross, was entirely powerless; although, in Jesus' case, this was not strictly true, for Jesus was only voluntarily powerless. As he put it to his disciples at the time of his arrest, "Do you think I cannot call on my Father, and he will at once put at my disposal more than twelve legions of angels?" (Matthew 26:53). Jesus chose this traumatic death. He *allowed* it to happen. He could at any point have brought it to an end but he chose not to. He experienced trauma in our place.

The Bible presents us with a God who knows the appalling experience of trauma from the inside. He has endured physical, emotional and spiritual agonies that we can only begin to guess about.

But there is still more to say. It isn't simply that Jesus understood trauma, nor even that he personally experienced

---

14 *The Cross of Christ* (IVP UK, 1986), p. 79.

it. These things certainly do make Jesus someone who can sympathise with our struggles (Hebrews 4:15), and there is much comfort in this. But the good news about Jesus goes so much further—for, by going to the cross, Jesus was doing far more than simply entering into our trauma. He was working to transform it.

Jesus transforms our trauma now

The Bible describes Jesus bearing the punishment for sin. In this he acts as our substitute—he takes our place, and he does what we would otherwise have had to do. He bears the punishment for our sin so that we don't have to.

But this swap works in both directions. Not only does he get what rightly belongs to us, but we also get what rightly belongs to him. "God made him who had no sin to be sin for us, so that in him we might become the righteousness of God" (2 Corinthians 5:21).

This is a salvation that brings glorious blessing. Trauma, as we have already seen, has far-reaching effects. Shame, isolation and damaged trust are just some of the relational consequences of trauma. Those who have been traumatised can feel desperately alone, desperately ashamed and utterly unable to enter into relationships of trust. Even the very best of friends (or therapists) may struggle to provide an adequate sense of safety for someone who has lived through trauma.

It is, therefore, of the greatest significance that when we come to Jesus, we find a Saviour who brings us an eternal safety. The psalms repeatedly describe the Lord as a refuge, shield and stronghold:

> "The LORD is a refuge for the oppressed, a stronghold in times of trouble." (Psalm 9:9)

"Show me the wonders of your great love, you who save by your right hand those who take refuge in you from their foes." (Psalm 17:7)

"The LORD is my rock, my fortress and my deliverer; my God is my rock, in whom I take refuge, my shield and the horn of my salvation, my stronghold."

(Psalm 18:2)

"The LORD is my strength and my shield; my heart trusts in him, and he helps me. My heart leaps for joy, and with my song I praise him." (Psalm 28:7)

"God is our refuge and strength, an ever-present help in trouble." (Psalm 46:1)

What Jesus promises is utterly different to anything that can be offered by another person. The refuge he provides comes from above. It is a stronghold in the heavens.

The love Jesus demonstrated on the cross speaks not only to our need for safety but also to our experiences of shame. And shame is frequently associated with trauma. As Ed Welch puts it, "Shame is the deep sense that you are unacceptable because of something you did, something done to you, or something associated with you. You feel exposed and humiliated."[15] It can leave a person feeling alienated—almost as if they don't deserve to be with other people. "You [feel you] are disgraced because you acted [as] less than human, you were treated as if you were less than human, or you were associated with something less than human, and there are witnesses."[16]

A victim of an assault, particularly a sexual assault, often feels sullied by what has been done to them. Military conflicts

---

15 *Shame Interrupted* (New Growth Press, 2012), Kindle loc. 142.
16 As above, loc. 144.

expose people to appalling atrocities, and witnessing or even participating in those events can have a long-lasting impact. Someone who has been through these kinds of experiences may feel damaged, compromised. A person can be told that they were not responsible and that they carry no guilt, yet those reassurances seem to carry no weight—their underlying sense of shame remains.

Events in a person's personal history are another source of shame—the suicide of a close family member or a dramatic breakdown in family relationships, for instance. People who have been adopted may also be prone to feelings of shame: "Even when their adoptive parents love them well, they can hear the message inside their heads, 'You were rejected. Somebody didn't want you. You are not like everyone else.'"[17]

When someone feels shame because of what they have done or because of what has been done to them, they become connected to an experience that, in some way or other, feels disgusting to them. And they want to hide.

But in contrast to a connection with that which feels shameful, the gospel connects us to Christ. Just as he reached out and touched lepers, Christ reaches out and touches us. In so doing, he receives us, accepts us and declares us worthy of connection even to his own self. Or, to use different biblical imagery, he clothes us: "All of you who were baptised into Christ have clothed yourselves with Christ" (Galatians 3:27). We are covered by his righteousness, meeting and overcoming the shame that makes us want to hide.

The gospel is gloriously personal. Jesus enters into relationship with us. He receives us—accepts us. He gives himself to us. Those affected by trauma are helped by a growing knowledge of this personal connection with Christ. Listening to him, speaking to him, joining with others in praise of

---

17 As above, loc. 290.

him—these are the central, and wonderful, elements of this deepening personal encounter.

In Christ we have, and can feel, safety—he is our refuge. In Christ we have, and can know, acceptance—he overcomes our shame (1 Peter 2:6). And in Christ, a sense of isolation is replaced by the experience of a constant companion who will never leave (Matthew 28:20; Hebrews 13:5).

To a person who has experienced trauma, and whose sense of safety has been profoundly disturbed, these are precious promises. They are not, of course, any kind of magical mantra. Simple repetition of these words is not a means to instant change. But these words are spoken to us in relationship. They are the words of the living God, who, in speaking them, invites us to believe him, trust him and put our faith in him. But the promises of Jesus aren't only a comfort in the here and now. They reach far further than that.

Jesus will transform our trauma in eternity

"In his great mercy he has given us new birth into a living hope through the resurrection of Jesus Christ from the dead, and into an inheritance that can never perish, spoil or fade. This inheritance is kept in heaven for you, who through faith are shielded by God's power until the coming of the salvation that is ready to be revealed in the last time." (1 Peter 1:3-5)

Peter says that the inheritance Jesus promises is "kept in heaven for you ... ready to be revealed in the last time". The Christian gospel is essentially future-orientated. It looks towards a hope yet to be revealed.

The language of transformation is rightly applied to this future hope. It concerns "a new heavens and a new earth" (2 Peter 3:13)—a new creation in which trauma will be a thing of the past. "'He will wipe every tear from their eyes.

There will be no more death' or mourning or crying or pain, for the old order of things has passed away" (Revelation 21:4, quoting from Isaiah 25:8).

This future hope is the driving force of the Christian faith, and a growing trust in the promise of all that God has in store for us transforms our experience of the present. Paul puts it in this way: "I consider that our present sufferings are not worth comparing with the glory that will be revealed in us" (Romans 8:18). The New Testament believers, including Paul, faced terrible persecution, yet saw those struggles in relation to "an eternal glory that far outweighs them all" (2 Corinthians 4:17).

None of this is intended to minimise the pain of the present or the profound impact of trauma into the future. Moving quickly through this gospel hope, as we have, risks suggesting that it is a quick and simple thing to bring gospel hope into the life of a person who has suffered trauma. It is neither of those things. The Bible never pretends that suffering is not real, nor that living in this world is easy. But this gospel hope is a real hope, and the comfort it brings is real comfort. And because these are found in a person, it means they are also found in relationship. But, like all relationships, a relationship with Christ takes time.

Caring for someone who is carrying trauma, then, must be centred on Christ. This means, first, that we need to depend on Christ for ourselves. Christ's wisdom and Christ's strength will be needed if we are to be effective helpers and companions for those in need. "Christ Jesus ... has become for us wisdom from God—that is, our righteousness, holiness and redemption" (1 Corinthians 1:30). It means, second, that we need to aim to be Christ-like in our care. When we care for others, we want to do so not just in his strength but also in his image: "In this world we are like Jesus" (1 John 4:17). When we are Christ-like in love, words about the grace of Christ are matched by actions and attitudes which communicate the same grace. And yet this means, third, that we will always seek to direct people away from ourselves and towards Jesus: "He is the one we proclaim, admonishing and teaching everyone with all wisdom, so that we may present everyone fully mature in Christ" (Colossians 1:28). We are not able to save anyone or change anyone. We do not need to pretend that we can, because we know the one who does—who is full of power and compassion and who moves towards those who are struggling.

As we listen to the promises of Christ, and believe in them, we find those promises trustworthy. More than that, we find *him* trustworthy. And as our confidence in him grows, so does our sense that there is a refuge where we are safe, a cover for our shame and a friend who will never leave us alone. So the best thing we can do as we navigate this life is to look to him—and to encourage others, however painful their situations, to look to him too.

Questions for reflection

1. Why do you think we seem to overlook the traumatic nature of many of the events described in the Gospel accounts?
2. What difficulties might exist in presenting the physical realities of the cross to those who have experienced severe suffering?
3. In considering the different challenges presented by feelings of fear, shame and isolation, many see shame as the hardest to deal with. Why might that be?

SECTION 2

CONTEMPORARY THINKING AND BIBLICAL PERSPECTIVES

SECTION 2

INTRODUCTION

The Bible, as we have seen, is not unfamiliar with the experience of trauma. Most importantly of all, the central event of the Christian faith—the cross—is itself a traumatic event. All this might lead us to expect that Bible-believing Christians are automatically well equipped to think about and respond to the experience of trauma.

The reality, however, is often far from that.

There are many reasons why Christians find engaging with trauma difficult. First, trauma disturbs and disrupts, and there is something in us that always wants to retreat from such experiences. We prefer not to have our sense of tranquillity disrupted, and we would rather our sense of safety remained undisturbed.

At its publication in 1992, Judith Herman's book *Trauma and Recovery* was identified as a groundbreaking work in the field of trauma studies. "To study psychological trauma," she observes, "is to come face to face both with human vulnerability in the natural world and with the capacity for evil in human nature. To study psychological trauma means bearing witness to horrible events."[18] We have a tendency to resist such disturbing encounters (which is one of the reasons why trauma victims can be disbelieved.)

Furthermore, the language used in trauma studies is unfamiliar to many church communities. Faced with terminology we do not understand and which we may struggle to

---

18 *Trauma and Recovery* (Basic Books, 1992), p. 7.

connect to the language of Scripture, there is a temptation to resist or retreat.

For this reason, the chapters in Section 2 of this book provide an outline of some of the key observations and theoretical frameworks described by those involved in trauma research. They are, inevitably, brief summaries, with complex issues set out in simple terms. Wherever possible, connections have been made to the concepts and language of Scripture. My hope, to use a phrase coined by Ed Welch, is to "normalise the abnormal" by trying to show how concepts that may feel abnormal and strange to many of us are connected to experiences with which we are already familiar.

I hope this will help Christians and churches gain confidence in engaging with those who have experienced trauma, particularly if they are using the language of trauma studies and trauma therapy to describe their experiences—and shape that engagement to be done with greater compassion and greater skill.

CHAPTER 6

HOW TRAUMA IS
UNDERSTOOD TODAY

"The ordinary response to atrocities is to banish them from consciousness. Certain violations ... are too terrible to utter aloud: this is the meaning of the word unspeakable."[19] This is the arresting opening to Judith Herman's study. All of us, probably, have on occasion described something as "unimaginably awful". "How unspeakably wicked," we might say, or "That's terrible—words fail me". Such phrases capture the idea that certain events can be so awful that we find ourselves unable to speak of them. They are beyond our comprehension. Yet this is more than a failure of imagination. Some things are so terrible that we don't *want* to speak about them. Something in us prefers to push atrocities out of our consciousness.

When trauma has been caused by a natural event, our resistance may connect to a sense of safety. We would rather not believe that the world can be so dangerous. When trauma has arisen from evil acts, our resistance takes a different form. We do not want to believe that people are capable of such evil because it disturbs our view of others and, indeed, of ourselves. We would rather believe that people have an essential goodness than that they are capable of acting in such heinous ways.

Yet by stating our belief that some things are "unspeakably awful", we are at least managing to say *something*. We have

19 As above, p. 1.

found some words to give mention to what has taken place. For many who are caught up directly in trauma, the experience is so overwhelming that words really do fail them.

Unspeakable (and "unhearable")

Our struggle to speak is often compounded by a struggle to hear. Given the choice, Herman notes, given the choice, we often prefer to believe the perpetrator rather than the victim. "All the perpetrator asks is that the bystander do nothing."[20] We wish to face no disturbance to the calm perception of the world that we have previously constructed: "A veil of oblivion is drawn over everything painful and unpleasant."[21] Perpetrators play upon this tendency; they rely on the desire to overlook and resist that which is uncomfortable, unpleasant and disturbing. "Secrecy and silence are the perpetrator's first line of defence. If secrecy fails, the perpetrator attacks the credibility of his victim."[22]

The victim, by contrast, cannot forget. They may well want to forget but, as we will see, the memory of what has happened refuses to be quiet. It continues to intrude. And when the trauma is eventually spoken about, it makes demands of others. The victim "asks the bystander to share the burden of pain. The victim demands action, engagement, and remembering."[23]

Understanding these elements in the dynamic of speaking about and hearing about trauma is vital, for unless we see and understand the way these powerful dynamics operate in our churches, they will be at work without us realising it and will render us liable to ignore those who have suffered trauma. Still worse, they may cause us to silence those who

---

20 As above, p. 7.
21 As above, p. 8.
22 As above, p. 8.
23 As above, p. 7.

are trying to find the courage to speak about the abuse they have suffered in church contexts.

Causes of trauma

The first part of this book will have shown you that there are many contexts in which trauma may be experienced. No list can be exhaustive, but it does help to realise that there are a very wide range of situations that can lead to people experiencing trauma (while remembering that experiencing a traumatic event does not necessarily mean that a person will suffer ongoing effects from that event):

- War and military conflict
- Natural disasters
- Road traffic accidents
- Child sexual abuse
- Criminal assault
- Domestic abuse
- Rape
- Controlling, coercive and bullying behaviour
- Racial discrimination
- Acute medical emergencies
- Chronic illness
- Forced migration
- Fire
- Bereavement

Some of the situations mentioned in this list are one-off events. Others involve contexts where trauma has been endured repeatedly for years. The latter will infuse people's experience from day to day. Growing up with such experiences means they become part of the very air a child breathes, and their impact reflects that.

Many of the examples listed above can, of course, occur in the context of church. In addition, many people identify a separate category of "spiritual abuse".

This term has proved contentious. To some, the existing categories of abuse are adequate to describe abuse that occurs in a religious context. Where someone acts in an emotionally or physically or sexually abusive way in a church, they would argue that those categories satisfactorily describe the abuse and that it only complicates things to add a separate category of spiritual abuse.

Others disagree. In their view, the spiritual context is significant and deserves to be noted. In church settings eternal issues are, of course, under consideration. When those in spiritual authority behave in coercive and controlling ways towards those under their pastoral care, they will often do so with threats about a person's spiritual status. The implication (or explicit message) is that unless a person complies with the leader's demands, their eternal destiny will be in doubt. Since the Bible encourages believers to submit to the authority of their leaders (Hebrews 13:7), it is easy to see the impact such threats can have.

Abuse which is cloaked in this kind of spiritual language can also be experienced in intimate relationships, particularly marriage. The distortion of Scripture to control and manipulate others in this way is particularly repulsive because of the way that it seeks to alienate the sufferer from the one true place of safety. Once this false view of God has been created, a person feels they have no one to turn to, for their very view of God himself has been distorted.

Even if much of the abuse which happens in a spiritual context can be adequately described by existing categories, this distinctive ability to cause a person to fear eternal damnation and to alienate them from God and the comfort of the gospel seems to many to justify a category of its own.

Some immediate responses to threat

In the face of threat, certain responses are intuitive and will be part of our common experience. If you have found yourself in the path of a rapidly approaching car, you may have had the strange experience of feeling rooted to the spot. Instead of hurrying to the safety of the pavement, we might *freeze*, motionless, like the proverbial rabbit in the headlights.

In other circumstances, however, we may experience being mobilised by threat. When pursued by a mugger, we find ourselves *fleeing* at speeds and for a length of time that we would never have imagined possible. This flight response attempts to remove us from threat.

These fight, flight and freeze responses are relatively well known. More recently, other responses have been added to this list.

- *Fawn* describes a submissive response in which a victim tries to placate an aggressor through compliance. Such responses are generally associated with situations involving long-standing threats and where escape is not possible.
- *Flop* is more extreme than freeze and typically involves the loss of bodily functions, leading a person to faint or in some sense mentally disconnect themselves from the threatening situation.
- By contrast a *fright* response describes the way in which a person can become hyper-aroused: incredibly attentive to their surroundings and able to absorb tiny details of the situation they face.

These six different responses to threat help us make sense of some of the features typically seen in a response to trauma.

There is no typical, predictable response to a traumatic event, and the way a person responds can also change over time. But a common one, and one that has gained increasing prominence in our everyday thinking and language, is PTSD—post-traumatic stress disorder.

Post-traumatic stress disorder

People struggle with their mental health in a wide range of ways. In order to identify and categorise these struggles, psychiatry has created detailed diagnostic classifications. These classifications identify the features which need to be present in order for a certain diagnostic category to be used. Such diagnoses are, therefore, descriptive rather than explanatory. They give a name to something that we experience.

PTSD is such a label. It describes a cluster of symptoms that are frequently seen in the aftermath of extreme suffering. Its emergence as a diagnostic category marked a very significant step in the development of trauma studies. In *The Body Keeps The Score*, Bessel van der Kolk describes how the experience of Vietnam veterans proved crucial to the development of this diagnosis. A turning point arrived in 1980, he comments, with the arrival of a new diagnosis:

> *"Systematically identifying the symptoms and grouping them together into a disorder finally gave a name to the suffering of people who were overwhelmed by horror and helplessness. With the conceptual framework of PTSD in place, the stage was set for a radical change in our understanding of patients. This eventually led to an explosion of research and attempts at finding effective treatments."*[24]

The features of PTSD can initially be confusing because

---

24 *The Body Keeps the Score*, p. 21.

some of the symptoms seem contradictory. Features that suggest a heightened sensitivity to stress exist alongside other features that involve numbing and distancing from people and situations. These apparent contradictions reflect a central dilemma in the experience of trauma. On the one hand, a person defends themselves against the horror of what has taken place—so they distance themselves from what has happened. They become numb.

On the other hand, those same events are so hard to comprehend that the mind resists attempts to force the memory of them under. Those memories return, unbidden, to consciousness like some terrible, unfinished story that demands a completion. No distance can be achieved, and no resolution can be found. The traumatised person therefore "finds herself caught between the extremes of amnesia or of reliving the trauma, between floods of intense, overwhelming feeling and arid states of no feeling at all, between irritable, impulsive action and complete inhibition of action."[25]

With that said, the features of PTSD are often summarised under three broad headings.

1. Hyperarousal

It makes sense that the experience of a traumatic event should cause a person to be hypersensitive to threat. This might be expressed in a heightened level of alertness and an awareness of potential danger. Early studies of "shell shock" identified a prominent startle reflex and pronounced hypervigilance. These remain central features in PTSD. People describe feeling "jumpy", and they may find themselves easily upset or quick to become angry. Persistent hyperarousal can also lead to psychosomatic complaints such as muscle and joint pain or digestive disorders.

---

25 *Trauma and Recovery*, p. 47.

2. Intrusion

When a person experiences a traumatic event, it seems to be recorded in a fractured form of memory. (We'll consider this in more detail in the next chapter.) Some think the language of memory is barely appropriate for the recollection of trauma. They suggest that the traumatic event, and the variety of physiological responses associated with that event, are held in some kind of unprocessed state. This incomplete processing, they suggest, means the event is liable to find its way back into consciousness either as flashbacks during waking hours or as traumatic nightmares during sleep.

These flashbacks are understood not so much as an experience of remembering but as a kind of re-experiencing of the traumatic event. It is as if what has happened is now happening all over again in the present moment. The same intensity of emotion and the same physical responses associated with the original trauma are re-experienced in the present. For some people these flashbacks or intrusive nightmares can be associated with a kind of re-enactment in which a person might exhibit the kind of aggressive or defensive actions that were needed in the original event.

People with such experiences may identify situations or stimuli which tend to precipitate these flashbacks. These precipitants are described as "triggers", and people who have experienced trauma will try to avoid these triggering stimuli.

3. Numbing

During a traumatic event, people may become detached from the events they are experiencing. This psychological distancing can be seen as a mechanism which protects a person against something unbearable. However, whatever the short-term benefits of this distancing mechanism, emotional numbing often becomes a problem in the aftermath of trauma.

Feeling emotionally numb and detached and with a lack of interest in activities that someone previously enjoyed is typical. This emotional numbness often creates significant relationship difficulties, and we will explore this further in chapter 8. Disturbance in memory, particularly in relation to the traumatic event itself, is also common, and we consider this in chapter 7.

In the aftermath of trauma, there is an increased use of alcohol and higher levels of drug dependency. The altered mental state created by the use of alcohol or drugs can be seen as a way of creating a kind of numbing in an effort to quieten some of the troubling effects of hyperarousal and intrusion. Other people use pornography to combat these experiences of hyperarousal.

Alongside this classic triad, several other features of PTSD are typically recognised. These include...

- sleep problems, which may be associated with hyper-arousal or caused by a fear of nightmares.
- mood changes: typically depression, which may also involve guilt, shame and self-blame.
- finding concentration difficult.
- feeling distant and detached from family and friends.

Dissociation

Experiences which involve a person feeling distanced or detached often come in the aftermath of a traumatic event. This is generally understood as a kind of numbing. It can provide an initial protection against experiences that threaten to overwhelm a person but may then recur as part of the ongoing impact of trauma.

Two kinds of dissociation are generally described. Depersonalisation involves feeling outside yourself. It may seem to a person that they are gazing down on themselves so that they become an observer of their own actions, feelings or thoughts. Someone may feel disconnected from parts of their body.

Derealisation is where the world feels unreal. People and things around a person feel distant or foggy. The person may feel separated from the world around them by a barrier of some kind, as if viewing the world through a pane of glass. Or they may feel as if they are in a dream.

Grounding techniques are different ways in which a person who is experiencing this kind of dissociation can re-connect with themselves and the world around them. Different exercises can help with this, and they include a person focusing on the feel of their feet on the floor and their body on the chair that they are sitting in. Moving their feet or body to accent those feelings is sometimes part of this exercise. Anxiety often rises when a person experiences this kind of dissociation—and grounding exercises are used to reduce levels of anxiety.

When people describe experiences that sound like dissociation, it is wise to recruit help and support from someone with experience in the management of this kind of anxiety.

Initial reflections

As we've already said, it is important to recognise that the impact trauma has on a person does bear some relationship to the severity of the trauma. The association is not, however, at all predictable. Two people experiencing an identical trauma can be affected in very different ways for reasons that are not always clear. For some, the symptoms of PTSD are dramatically disabling. Others experience milder versions of these symptoms.

Again, as with the word "trauma" itself, many experts working in this field have begun to express concern at the way the terminology of PTSD has been adopted to describe experiences that might better be identified as mildly troubling rather than in any sense traumatic. Again, this "concept creep" risks invalidating the very considerable struggles experienced by those who have faced suffering at the more extreme end of the spectrum.

Nevertheless, PTSD has become a more common diagnosis in the past couple of decades, and it is likely that some in your church are struggling with it, perhaps without feeling able to tell anyone about it. Having outlined what PTSD is, it's time to provide a little more detail about three key areas in the experience of trauma—first, the way memories are processed in trauma; second, the effects of trauma on the body; and third, the impact trauma has on relationships.

Questions for reflection

1. Trauma is not just hard to speak about; it is also hard to hear about. Can you imagine (or remember) not wanting to hear about another person's suffering?
2. As you look at the list of possible causes of trauma, which might you not have thought to include, and why?
3. "The features of PTSD can, initially, be confusing because some of the symptoms seem contradictory" (page 79). Which elements of the usual responses to trauma seem least obvious to you?

CHAPTER 7

TRAUMA AND MEMORY

Bessel van der Kolk describes an encounter from the early stages of his work in trauma with a disturbed man who, his colleagues were convinced, was suffering from a psychotic breakdown. Yet he was not convinced:

> *"Something about the diagnosis didn't sound right. I asked Bill if I could talk with him, and after hearing his story, I unwittingly paraphrased something Sigmund Freud had said about trauma in 1895: I think this man is suffering from memories."*[26]

A mind overwhelmed

Central to understanding the impact of trauma is the way extreme suffering is simply too much for a person to cope with. Trauma involves "intense fear, helplessness, loss of control, and threat of annihilation".[27] Such experiences overwhelm someone's normal capacity to cope. Nothing in their prior experience has prepared them either to comprehend or to navigate what is happening: "The essence of trauma is that it is overwhelming, unbelievable, and unbearable".[28]

A traumatic event bombards a person not just with external stimuli—sights, sounds, feel and smell—but also with their own internal sensory experience. Feelings of panic,

---

26 *The Body Keeps the Score*, p. 17.
27 *Trauma and Recovery*, p. 33.
28 *The Body Keeps the Score*, p. 235.

terror and dread may all be part of their response to what is happening. In normal situations of danger and threat, we are preparing either to defend ourselves or to flee, and our bodily responses mobilise us to respond. One of the key features of trauma, however, is helplessness—a person can neither resist nor escape. This is understood to be central to the physiological and psychological impact of trauma.

In the aftermath of this experience of helplessness, it seems as if these bodily responses persist. So a person exists in a hyperaroused state, fully prepared for action but unable to take any. This seems to cause disruption of normally connected responses—memories and emotions get separated: "The human system of self-defence becomes overwhelmed and disorganized ... Traumatic events may sever these normally integrated functions from one another. The traumatized person may experience intense emotion but without clear memory of the event, or may remember everything in detail but without emotion."[29]

Fragments of memory

Standard memories appear to be recorded in narrative form: they have a beginning, a middle and an end. When such memories are recalled, they maintain this narrative form. Over time, these memories are also affected by the retelling. Some parts are emphasised while others are gradually forgotten. All this is a usual part of memory formation and recall.

The memory of traumatic events seems to be distinctly different. The disorganising and disrupting impact of sensory overload means the imprint that arises as a result of trauma seems to consist of something more like isolated fragments—snatches of sensory experience which are locked in time and have not been organised into any kind

---

29 *Trauma and Recovery*, p. 34.

of narrative whole. This imprint often includes emotional experiences that were associated with the original event. The recall of trauma, therefore, may involve a disturbingly disorganised set of isolated sensory experiences. A particular smell or touch may be connected with certain powerful emotions, such as dread or fear, as well as a series of bodily sensations that accompanied the original trauma.

This essentially fragmentary form of traumatic memory is thought to be connected to the experience of flashbacks, when a person does not so much remember an event as relive it:

> *"I want to tell you what a flashback is like. It is as if time is folded or warped, so that the past and present merge, as if I were physically transported into the past. Symbols related to the original trauma, however benign in reality, are thoroughly contaminated and so become objects to be hated, feared, destroyed if possible, avoided if not."* [30]

Someone who experienced sexual abuse as a young child may have no organised memory of the event. In that sense, they do not "remember" it at all. This is one explanation for why memories of abuse sometimes only emerge into consciousness during counselling or therapy. Yet even when a traumatic event is not remembered, it can still be evoked. The smell of the aftershave used by an abuser might trigger an intense emotional reaction, as well as stirring bodily sensations which cause a person to act in inexplicable ways. In the absence of a narrative memory of the event, the response will be as mysterious to others as it usually is to the person themselves.

---

30 *The Body Keeps the Score*, p. 238.

Stories matter

We tell stories to make sense of our lives. In general, when we describe ourselves and our past to others, we use narratives. If someone has experienced extreme suffering and lacks this narrative structure in their memory of the event, it can be impossible to integrate it into their sense of themselves and their past. Traumatic memories have been likened to a series of still photos or a silent movie. Recovery is described as a process in which a person finds words and music to go alongside these wordless images.[31]

In the broadest terms, supporting someone through this process is understood to involve three steps. First, there is the need to establish a safe and secure setting in which to begin the process of remembering. Second is the process of recalling. Slowly and carefully over a period of time, the traumatic event is recalled in order that it can be integrated into a person's broader life story. The third phase involves establishing a new way forward in relationship with individuals and community and in which the experience of trauma is now an integrated part.

Of course, the paragraph above hardly begins to capture the complexity of all that this process may involve. Different people will experience this "remembering" in very different ways. A key element, however, is retelling the story in a way that begins to attach the events to the relevant emotions. A factual recollection of traumatic events from the past that is not associated with the emotional impact arising from the events is unlikely to help someone achieve progress.

It may also be important to help a person notice aspects of the story of their trauma that have so far been overlooked. Perhaps there were moments when they demonstrated a

---

31 See *Trauma and Recovery*, p. 174.

right determination to resist what was happening or when they offered help to others who were being affected. A fuller story of their trauma may then be created, which includes positive elements and is less bleak and hopeless than the one that existed previously.

Here is one illustration of how this might look. A man whose child had experienced a life-threatening medical emergency found himself unable to engage with medical appointments or hospitals without beginning to feel both overcome and out of control. He would experience this in a distinct way. There would be a sense of distancing from the present moment. He would feel physically dissociated from his surroundings—a kind of numbing. At other times, he could experience intense anxiety with feelings of dread and threat—a kind of hyperarousal. Such experiences could take him unawares. They might arise unexpectedly in a way that mystified him until he realised that he was driving on a road that led to his local hospital. This was an experience of intrusion, where his location was triggering his fragmented memory.

Over several meetings, and in the context of a broader discussion about the Bible's teaching on the place of suffering in the Christian life and the psalmist's emotional engagement with God, a general picture of what had happened was established. This was the phase in which a sense of safety and security and trust was created, and he was able to decide what he was ready to talk about.

That being done, he was able to speak in detail about the life-threatening events involving his child. During this re-telling, the intensity of his emotional engagement was clear. Revisiting the events did not feel like remembering. For him, it was as though he was reliving what had taken place. The intensity of emotion he felt during this recounting of events took him by surprise, as did finding himself remembering tiny details of the original incidents—many of them things about which he had previously been unaware. He became able to notice the many ways he had responded thoughtfully and lovingly—he wasn't as helpless as he had thought. His actions had been both significant and important.

One of the difficulties in his experience of trauma was that he and his wife had responded in very different ways to their son's illness. These differences and his own inability to talk about what had happened with anyone, including his wife, had led to an increasing disruption in their marriage.

Narratives, psalms and remembering

In this light, the prominence of Old Testament narratives which record suffering and struggle is striking. The Old Testament people of God were enslaved, besieged and exiled. They experienced drought and famine. As a nation, they faced recurrent hardship and difficulty. A striking aspect of their response to these struggles is that they told stories about them. The historical books of the Old Testament provide detailed narrative accounts of wars and sieges, exiles and defeats. Several psalms, moreover, set out these experiences in poetic form:

- Psalm 78 revisits the experience of the exodus more than once, before moving to an account of the ark of the covenant being taken into captivity. In this revisiting of tragic and traumatic events, the failing of the people is often emphasised. They "spoke against God; they said, 'Can God really spread a table in the wilderness?'" (v 19). "They would flatter him with their mouths, lying to him with their tongues … they put God to the test and rebelled against the Most High" (v 36, 56). Both the terrible things that happened and the people's own part in the tragedy that unfolded are emphasised.

- Psalm 105 not only relates the devastating events that befell God's people but also the suffering of specific individuals, such as Joseph (v 17-22).
- Psalm 106 recounts the events of the Exodus, and then includes verses describing the rebellion recounted in Numbers 25 when the people "yoked themselves to the Baal of Peor" (Psalm 106:28) and a plague broke out against them.
- Psalms 135 and 136 also summarise events from the history of Israel. Psalm 135 emphasises how God has been sovereign over this history, contrasting the rule of God with the idols of the nations who are powerless, having mouths that cannot speak and eyes that cannot see (Psalm 135:15-18). Psalm 136 records parts of Israel's history using a series of brief stanzas each of which concludes with the recurring refrain: "His love endures for ever".

Through these Scriptures, God ensured that his people's history would always be prominent in their communal memory. They would know the trials and struggles that their ancestors had endured. It was part of the lived experience of their people. They would also have been clear about the way that sinful rebellion had contributed to the devastating judgments that unfolded. These things were known and understood and retained in the nation's cultural memory.

Greater and lesser experiences of suffering

There may, perhaps, be more than one way that this cultural remembering enables God's people to endure suffering and struggle. Some argue, for example, that the remembering of severe suffering in the past helps a community to be more resilient in the present.

In a chapter about the historical nature of PTSD, Richard McNally says:

> *"People whose understanding of trauma has been shaped by the horrors of World War II (Snyder 2010), including having survived Nazi death factories, such as Treblinka ... are unlikely to be much affected by [some of] the stressors ... that can apparently cause PTSD today. Perhaps one unfortunate consequence of the otherwise undeniable benefits of modernity is diminished resilience. Our relatively greater comfort, safety, health, and well-being may have rendered us more vulnerable to stressors far less toxic than the ones occurring during World War II for example."*[32]

By revisiting the horrors of the past, the biblical accounts ensured that the suffering experienced by God's people was held in their cultural memory. Perhaps this process served some kind of protective function. Recalling severe struggles in the past will sometimes put present difficulties into perspective.

Researchers speak about intergenerational trauma, where trauma that has affected one generation also seems to impact their children and grandchildren. Perhaps, in a more positive way, some sort of protective function might also be transmitted across the generations. Present-day believers are only distantly connected with the generations of God's people whose suffering is captured in the Bible. Yet their experiences are identified as "examples", "encouragements"

---

32 Richard McNally, "Is PTSD a Transhistorical Phenomenon?" in Devon E. Hinton, Byron J. Good, Devon E. Hinton, Byron J. Good (eds), *Culture and PTSD: Trauma in Global and Historical Perspective* (University of Pennsylvania Press, 2015), p. 129-130.

and "warnings" for us today (1 Corinthians 10:11; Romans 15:4). By reminding ourselves that "our relatively greater comfort, safety, health and well-being" is not guaranteed, we are not so easily taken by surprise when hardship comes.

Having said all that, we must always remember that there are experiences of suffering that *should* be felt and should *not* be minimised. Certain kinds of extreme suffering merit grief and outrage, and it would be wrong if such a response was not forthcoming in those circumstances. Biblical Christianity is not stoic. When people face extreme suffering and struggle as a result, we must not automatically convey the impression that we think this is due to some kind of failure in faith or a result of poor theology. It is not necessarily either of those things. Some things deserve, even demand, outrage and upset—just as they do in the biblical narrative.

Questions for reflection

1. Do you have any memories that are unusually vivid (or unusually vague) because they are recollections of particularly difficult events?

2. In a flashback, "it is as if time is folded or warped, so that the past and present merge, as if I were physically transported into the past". What do you think would be most disturbing about such an experience?

3. Does it make sense to you that recalling suffering in the past could make an experience of suffering in the present somehow less distressing?

CHAPTER 8

TRAUMA AND THE BODY

In *Mental Health and Your Church*, I described how my undergraduate studies in neuropharmacology included a particularly striking moment.[33] The lecturer, despite being at the very forefront of her field, wanted to emphasise how much we did not know about the brain and its functioning. The complexity of the brain, she observed, and the lack of specificity of the drugs we have available to bring about changes in our neurochemistry is such that our current efforts to treat psychiatric disorders by using medication is something like a car mechanic trying to fix a faulty car by hitting the engine with a hammer!

In the 40 years since she made that remark, our understanding of the complexity of the human brain has only increased—but the range and specificity of the drugs available to us have not altered fundamentally. Yet at present, a biological approach to mental health problems still predominates. This reflects the current tendency to pay more attention to the material than to the immaterial. Body, rather than soul, has our attention.

This chapter will provide a brief summary of theoretical approaches to trauma that emphasise its biological basis. Yet articulating a theory for the biological basis of trauma can never provide a comprehensive understanding of what happens when a person is impacted by trauma. We are more

---

33 Steve Midgley and Helen Thorne, *Mental Health and Your Church* (The Good Book Company, 2023), p. 44.

than our biology and we are more than our brains. We live in an age when biological reductionism (the idea that there is nothing more to us than our material selves) is a dominant philosophical framework. From that vantage point, it is a small step to imagine that once we have understood what is happening in our brains, we will have arrived at a full and sufficient explanation of things. This perspective will tend to lead us to interventions that have biological rather than psychological or, indeed, spiritual foundations.

Interestingly, Bessel van der Kolk is himself clear about the limitations of biological approaches:

> *"The drug revolution that started out with so much promise may in the end have done as much harm as good. The theory that mental illness is caused primarily by chemical imbalances in the brain that can be corrected by specific drugs has become broadly accepted, by the media and the public as well as by the medical profession ... I have come to realise that psychiatric medications have a serious downside, as they may deflect attention from dealing with the underlying issues. The brain-disease model takes control over people's fate out of their own hands and puts doctors and insurance companies in charge of fixing their problems."*[34]

Given their prominence, it is important to be aware of the neuroscientific theories currently dominating the field of trauma studies—but we should do so with an understanding of the provisional nature of all scientific theory.

A note about scientific theories

The history of science makes clear that scientific theories must always be considered to be provisional. As science

---

34 *The Body Keeps the Score*, p. 42.

advances, things that were once "obviously" true become inadequate explanations of reality. Our forebears believed there were four cardinal "humours" (or fluids) in our bodies—blood, phlegm, choler (yellow bile) and melancholy (black bile)—and the relative balance of these humours was believed to determine someone's temperament. That theoretical framework is reflected in the way we still sometimes describe people as sanguine (the Latin for blood is *sanguis*), phlegmatic, choleric (quick to anger) or melancholic.

Scientific theories also direct the treatments we use. The "humoural theory" identified imbalances in body fluids. An obvious treatment, therefore, was to extract some fluid in order to restore the elusive balance. Blood-letting was one such treatment, and the application of leeches is how it was generally achieved. It first gained widespread popularity through the writings of Galen in the 2nd century, but the practice persisted for centuries. An established medical textbook still mentioned blood-letting as a treatment for pneumonia as recently as 1935![35]

Today no serious scientist believes that our illnesses are related to imbalances in four fundamental humours. Yet there was a time when that did seem clear, obvious and true. It requires a certain cultural arrogance to suppose that contemporary theories will somehow prove immune to this ongoing advance of scientific knowledge. Much of what we currently consider to be cutting-edge science will presumably be overturned in much the same way as the theories of previous generations.

This does not mean that the theories which describe the impact of trauma on the basis of changes in the anatomy of the brain should be dismissed or ignored. Science advances

---

35 Timothy Bell, "A Brief History of Bloodletting" in *The Journal of Lancaster General Hospital*, 2016, Vol 11, No4.

through the development of theories. They provide the basis for ongoing study and research. As theories are refined, our understanding progresses. It is important, however, to remember what scientific theories are, and what they are not. They are hypotheses about the way reality may work which offer a way to understand and explain what we observe, but they are only ever provisional.

The language and terminology used in scientific theories also affects how we speak. At their best, they provide metaphorical images to help put complicated experiences into words. However, theories can become unduly solid in our thinking, as if they were facts rather than possibilities. David Powlison, who worked as the Executive Director of CCEF (the Christian Counseling and Educational Foundation), used an "upstream, downstream" analogy to describe how this can affect us. He identified those who are "upstream" as the people at the forefront of their field. These individuals are working close to the source of the stream, where the water is pure and clear. Their thinking and writing is clear, and they understand the provisional nature of the theories they are proposing and see all the complexity of the phenomena they are studying. Once the water has travelled some distance "downstream", however, it becomes cloudy, even muddy. Downstream, things are not nearly so well understood—theory has become fact, complexities are overlooked and the provisional nature of those theories is ignored.

Downstream, complicated experiences get expressed in ways that are an oversimplification. Treatments which are provisional become unquestionable dogmas. We should anticipate that some of the treatments we value today will eventually turn out to be the modern equivalent of blood-letting. Our problem, of course, is that we don't yet know which ones will prove to be that.

What follows below is an (inevitably simplified) account of the trauma theories that our culture increasingly uses to describe and understand the experience of trauma. Rather like the ideas of Freud from a former generation, this theoretical framework is finding its way into popular consciousness. Few people who may identify misplaced words as a Freudian slip will ever have read any of Sigmund Freud's theoretical writings. Similarly, when people today speak about "the limbic system" or our "mammalian brain", they do so without awareness of the theoretical thinking underpinning these ideas.

A neuroscientific theory of trauma
1. The triune brain

The triune brain theory describes the human brain as having three distinct elements, each serving a different function and each with a different evolutionary status.[36] The "reptilian brain", the deepest layer, is understood to be our primitive brain. It is said to be rigid, obsessive, and ritualistic. It controls autonomic functions such as breathing, sleeping and heart rate.

What is described as the "mammalian brain" is the next level up and is made up of components that are together termed the "limbic system". This part of the brain is said to be concerned with emotions and behaviours that connect us with others socially. This includes activities such as feeding, fighting, fleeing and our sexual activity.

The outermost layer, known as the neocortex or "new brain", is understood to be the most recent part of the brain in evolutionary terms. It is said to be uniquely human and is

---

36 The theory was first proposed by Paul MacLean in the 1960s and was popularised by Carl Sagan in his book *The Dragons of Eden* (Ballantine Books, 1989).

concerned with cognition and rational thought. One part of the neocortex, the prefrontal cortex, is identified as having a particular role in regulating the mammalian and reptilian brains. The neocortex, then, is said to exert rational control over our more primitive and animalistic tendencies.

This theoretical framework shows striking similarities to previous theories about human functioning. In ancient Greece, Plato theorised about powerful instincts and emotions, which he believed needed to be controlled by rational thought. There are also echoes of the psychodynamic ideas of Sigmund Freud, whose conflict theory of human motivation was based on a struggle between a primitive id, a restrictive super-ego and some kind of relational compromise determined by the ego.

The idea that people are pulled by competing forces is a consistent theme across many attempts to explain human experience, not least in Scripture itself. The Bible describes sin as a force that is seeking to master us. God warns Cain that "sin is crouching at your door; it desires to have you, but you must rule over it" (Genesis 4:7). The apostle Paul describes our experiences as a choice between two competing slaveries: "Don't you know that when you offer yourselves to someone as obedient slaves, you are slaves of the one you obey—whether you are slaves to sin, which leads to death, or to obedience, which leads to righteousness?" (Romans 6:16). The triune brain theory is, perhaps, best understood as an imperfect reflection of spiritual realities—realities that are set out for us in the Bible's description of what it is to be people living this side of the fall.

2. Brain functioning in response to danger

Evolutionary theory leads us to believe that a survival instinct will be a high priority for any organism. This would cause us to expect that being alert to danger and threat will be important for us. The faster we can detect and respond to threat, the better our chances of survival will be. In situations of threat, such as those which happen in trauma, the brain detects danger and responds by preparing the body for action. This response is best known in terms of "fight or flight" (which, as we've seen, is often now expanded to include freeze, fawn, flop and fright). Physiological changes cause our senses to focus on the source of threat and prime our muscles to act. Our heart rate increases and our breathing becomes rapid. This response is understood to be associated with the two more primitive parts of the brain—the reptilian part, which activates physiological responses, and the limbic system, which is responsible for us feeling scared. This response has been likened to the functioning of a smoke alarm.[37]

If an assailant jumps out of a darkened alley directly in front of us, our body responds by moving into this alert mode. We are ready to engage in resistance, or we are ready to turn and flee. The neurological pathways causing this response work at high speed—these processes happen before any conscious appraisal of the threat has taken place. In this sense, they are an instinctive response.

However, a second process is also understood to take place. A slower pathway ("slow" here is a relative term since we are talking about a few more milliseconds!) processes the incoming sensory data at a more cognitive level. This process involves the prefrontal cortex, where the sensory data is appraised and compared with past experiences to arrive at a more considered judgement about what is happening in the world around us. This response has been likened to a watch tower because it has a broader, fuller view of what is going on.[38]

---

37 *The Body Keeps the Score*, p. 70.
38 As above, p. 72.

Suppose, for example, that even as our body tenses and trembles with a flood of adrenaline, our sensory systems hear the word "surprise" and see a balloon with the words "Happy Birthday" on it. Our secondary, slower pathway transfers this data to the rational, thinking part of our brain and connects it with the fact that it is indeed our birthday and that the face in front of us is not an assailant but an old friend who has decided to surprise us. Our rational brain moves us from threat mode to calm mode. However, adrenaline is already in our system, and this calming takes time. "Wow, you gave me quite a shock," we might say, as our jangling nerves gradually begin to settle.

3. Altered brain function following trauma

Definitions of trauma, as we saw in chapter 2, emphasise the experience of helplessness. Somatic theories which emphasise our bodily responses understand that a person facing a traumatic event is subject to two conflicting experiences. On the one hand, they are experiencing a powerful fight/flight response, but on the other hand, their helplessness means they are unable to action either of those responses. They might be trapped in a war zone, unable to flee, or pinned down by an assailant who is physically far more powerful than they are. The person can neither flee nor fight back. Sometimes this inability to respond might be more psychological than physical. A person might have reason to believe that fighting back will cause harm to someone else—where an abusive husband is threatening to harm his wife's children, for instance. Or perhaps a person fears that resistance will lead to them being punished—for example, in a situation where an abusive spiritual leader claims divine authority and tells church members that to resist them is to defy God or deny the gospel.

When someone experiences trauma, it is understood to

create lasting changes to their neurophysiology. Having been in an aroused state but unable to act on that arousal changes their brain functioning. The changes are described in terms of a disturbance in the balance between the primitive threat-detection system and the more sophisticated cognitive appraisal. We might say that the smoke detector is supersensitive, and the watch tower can't seem to switch it off.

As a result of this, when certain things happen in the world—such as a soldier hearing a firework—the threat-detection system is quickly and vigorously activated ("I'm under attack"), but the rational appraisal ("It's okay; it's only a firework") does not function normally and so cannot restore a sense of calm. The person therefore experiences a prolonged stress response—more like reliving the experience than remembering it. This is a "flashback", which has been "triggered" by whatever reminded them of the original threat.

Researchers have conducted experiments in which they have induced flashbacks in people while monitoring them in brain scanners. The scanners measure changes in the flow of blood in different parts of the brain, and this suggests that during a flashback, there is reduced activity in the prefrontal cortex and increased activity in structures associated with the limbic system. This is interpreted as a kind of "switching off" of the rational brain in favour of the "emotional brain".

4. Brain functioning and memory

These theories are also used to suggest a basis for the changes in memory that we considered in the previous chapter. Organised memories, it is supposed, take the form of a completed story. An incident from the past is recorded as a kind of episode with a beginning, middle and end. If trauma disturbs the proper functioning of the rational part of the brain, which includes the processing of language, then perhaps this might also disrupt the creation of normal memories. The incident might be "remembered" only in terms of emotional and sensory experiences and without the verbal or rational meaning required for a cogent, organised memory. This, it is suggested, might leave the person vulnerable to revisiting the past in a way that is largely sensory and emotional rather than as a normal narrative remembering of what took place.

Responding to the theories: some positives

These theories offer those suffering from the bewildering impact of trauma a way to make sense of their experiences. After trauma, the past intrudes into the present in unwelcome ways, and people do feel themselves to be in a constant state of high alert for no reason. A theory that explains those experiences and shows how someone has been affected by events in the past can be a relief. It means they are not irrationally out of control or acting in bizarre ways for no good reason. They are given a biological explanation for what is happening to them.

Moreover, that explanation makes intuitive sense. The idea is that something can be so far beyond normal experience that a person's ability to comprehend it is overwhelmed. That has an intrinsic logic. The idea that this event hasn't been absorbed or integrated like other events also makes sense. It provides an explanation for why the event keeps surfacing in the present.

"So, my smoke alarm is oversensitive? That's why I overreact to things sometimes?"

"My calming watch-tower response has been silenced— does that explain why I feel on edge all the time?"

It's easy to see how such vivid imagery can help a person gain a sense of order in the face of experiences that are proving to be enormously troubling.

These theories have also highlighted the important role the body has in the experience of trauma. For some time now, Western culture has prized the role of thought in making sense of, and correcting, our troubles. This neuro-scientific theory of trauma explains how thoughts can be disempowered, rendering them unable to quieten the stress and alarm that a person is feeling. It also explains how alarm is experienced in the body and invites us to pay more attention to the workings of our physical frame, which, arguably, has been neglected in favour of the mind.

Finally, this theoretical framework invites us to consider how physical interventions might be of value. It provides a basis for interventions that might be described as from bottom up (from body to mind) rather than from top down (from mind to body).[39]

Some concerns

Connecting the impact of trauma with changes in brain structures can, however, feel disempowering: "If this is something that has happened to me, so that the very structure of my brain has been altered, how will I ever recover?" Any approach that takes a radically reductionist view—in other words, that believes we are nothing more than our material selves—risks creating a kind of passivity. One writer suggests that "the wounding of trauma could be considered a form of brain injury" and that "this psychological trauma wounding takes the survivor beyond the capabilities of talking therapies".[40] This disempowering can also extend to family and

---

39 As above, p. 3.
40 Joanna Naomi Douglas, *Building a Trauma-Informed Worshipping Community*

friends who want to support those affected by trauma but cannot see how that is possible if the problem is a material change in the brain. It can seem as if the complexity of what has taken place puts people beyond the care of an ordinary church family. There is certainly a need for understanding and wisdom in the church—that is the premise behind this book—but if the complexity of theoretical frameworks only creates a "hands off, steer clear" attitude among churches, we will have misstepped.

Of course, it need not be like this. It is entirely possible to conceive of how our relationships and our communities can use language and meaning to bring about healing and how that healing can include physiological change.[41]

Remember, when theories get downstream they lose their provisional nature and become absolute. We "have a triune brain"; "my prefrontal cortex just switches off, and I lose rational thought". Yet these are theories, open to further development and even to being refuted. And the field of neuroscience is not of one mind on this matter. Lisa Feldman Barrett, a leading neuroscientist, has written a book called *Seven and a Half Lessons about the Brain*. In it she makes this comment: "The triune brain idea is one of the most successful and widespread errors in all of science. It's certainly a compelling story, and at times, it captures how we feel in daily life ... But human brains don't work that way. Bad behavior doesn't come from ancient and unbridled beasts. Good behavior is not the result of rationality. And rationality and emotion are not at war ... they do not even live in separate parts of the brain."[42]

Some measure of scepticism, without abandoning an in-

(Grove Books, 2023), p. 9, 4.

41 *The Body Keeps the Score*, p. 44.

42 *Seven and a Half Lessons about the Brain* (Picador, 2020), p. 15-16.

terest in theoretical ideas, is warranted. We would do well to approach trauma with an interest in what is observable. We should also do so without losing confidence in the idea that wise and thoughtful care from the people of God remains relevant and important. Some people have an over-reliance on neuroscientific theories. Others are determined to dismiss them completely. Either of those attitudes can cause us to miss the person in front of us and fail to engage with them as we should.

The impact of trauma on relationships is fundamental because relationships are fundamental. We are social beings, made by God to live in community. As we shall see in the next chapter, trauma can have a profoundly disruptive impact on relationships. But as we shall also see, relationships are profoundly important in the care, support and recovery of those affected by trauma.

Questions for reflection

1. What do you find most compelling about the secular theories of trauma that are set out in this chapter?
2. Do you agree that these theories about brain changes may lead to an attitude of passivity in a person? How do you think we can resist that happening?
3. Are you aware of the tendency (either in yourself or others) of treating scientific theories as if they were actually facts?

CHAPTER 9

TRAUMA AND RELATIONSHIPS

There is something in our conversations about trauma that seems to push us towards a very individualistic perspective. We identify a traumatised *person*. *He* faced a terrible experience of suffering, and it affected him. *She* is now someone suffering with post-traumatic stress. Yet this tendency to think and speak in such individualistic terms risks contributing to one particularly troubling impact of trauma—that of feeling profoundly alone.

Helplessness is an invariable element in the experience of trauma. A person not only feels unable to help themselves but also isolated from outside help. No one comes close. The things they have faced are unspeakably bad, and the absence of speech produces barriers that prevent others from even being told of the awfulness of what has taken place. Without being able to convey their experience of harm, they are alone with their suffering.

God has made us as relational beings, reflecting his own relational, triune nature. Considering the way trauma affects a person's relationships is crucial if we are to understand the full impact that trauma has on a person. More positively, things work in the opposite direction as well. We need to think relationally because relationships and community play a central role in recovery from trauma.

Judith Herman puts it like this: "Helplessness and isolation are the core experiences of psychological trauma.

Empowerment and reconnection are the core experiences of recovery."[43]

Those involved in trauma research describe the key role played by the community that exists around a person impacted by trauma. It is not difficult to see the implications for the role a local church can play in trauma recovery. The qualities God intends to be embodied within the community of the church are uniquely suited to the care and restoration of those affected by trauma.

So let's consider the way trauma does damage both to a person's relationships and their connections with the wider community, and outline some of the ways that a community's attitudes and behaviour can exacerbate the harm done by trauma, so that we can then start to see the many ways in which a church community can provide care and support that work towards the restoration of those affected by trauma.

The relational impact of trauma

Isolation is a central experience in trauma. The extreme nature of the suffering involved places the person in a category that feels unique: *Others haven't experienced what I have experienced—how can they ever understand what it was like? And I don't have words to describe it to them—I can't seem to help them see what it was like.*

Helplessness adds to the sense of isolation. There was no one to call to for help. Or perhaps there were people to call to, but a response was not forthcoming. People did not seem able, or willing, to hear the cries for help.

In situations of abuse, a demand for silence is often a feature of the power exerted by the perpetrator over their victim. *Let's make this our little secret. Others won't understand. No one*

---

43 *Trauma and Recovery*, p. 197.

will believe you. A person in a situation of abuse may have been isolated for years.

Loss of trust is another common relational casualty in trauma. The world no longer feels safe. The ability of others to keep us secure was once assumed—but that no longer seems true. An expectation of care may be replaced by an expectation of threat. A person's sense of security is disturbed, even broken.

At a spiritual level, trauma may lead to a crisis of faith. *What was God doing? Why didn't he protect me? How could he have left me all alone? Can God really be good if things like this can happen?*

Where a person has suffered abuse in a spiritual setting, trust in the institution of the church is likely to have been severely affected. Those in positions of authority are no longer a source of comfort and security—quite the reverse. The community that God intends to be a place of security, love and grace has instead become a context for threat and harm.

Many will enter a church building filled with a sense of belonging. Those who have experienced abuse, especially where it has happened in a church setting, are more likely to feel as if they are entering enemy territory, where they must be alert and on guard. As they enter a church building, it is not with a sense of peace but with profound unease and hypervigilance.

Shame, as we've already seen, is commonly experienced by those who have experienced trauma. Being in a position of helplessness can itself feel shaming. An inability to help yourself and a sense that you have not been able to manage what happened to you can leave a person feeling like a failure or in some sense inadequate. If what happened involved an indignity of some sort, the sense of shame is often intensified.

When someone has been traumatised in the context of war, they may feel shame about what they have done or what they failed to do. Victims of sexual assault have a very distinctive experience of shame: "The purpose of the attack is precisely to demonstrate contempt for the victim's autonomy and dignity ... shame is a response to helplessness, the violation of bodily integrity, and the indignity suffered in the eyes of another person".[44]

Making things worse

The sense of isolation and shame felt by someone who has experienced trauma is intensified when their community proves uncomprehending. That community could be society at large or a more specific community, such as church or family. Sometimes a community is unwilling to listen to those who have experienced trauma. What has happened may seem too difficult or too complicated or too disturbing. Listening may require a shift of perspective that the community is determined to resist, or it may require some specific action that the community is unwilling to perform.

This may lead a community to minimise or even directly refute the account told to them. Minimisation and denial are more likely if the account of trauma has implications for those in positions of authority and power. Victims of sexual abuse often face powerful institutional resistance when they try to make known what has happened to them. This has been the recent experience of those who have exposed abuse both in the church and in the entertainment industry.

When a victim has found the courage to speak and is still not heard or believed, they feel even more isolated and alone. Suggestions that they are exaggerating what has

---

44 As above, p. 53.

happened, or at the very least are being oversensitive, only add to their sense of shame.

These responses reinforce the sense that the world is not safe. People are not proving trustworthy or reliable. The cry for help is not heard, and no one comes to offer aid. Feelings of helplessness and lost trust are intensified.

When a church fails to respond to someone who has experienced trauma or where it responds by minimising or even deriding someone's experience, those attitudes can come to be associated with God. If his people don't want to hear, perhaps God doesn't want to either. If his people won't help, presumably nor will God. If even my Christian community is ashamed of me, there really must be something to be ashamed about.

Bringing support and healing

Responses that offer support and healing are the inverse of those just outlined. This involves a community listening to accounts of suffering and seeking to fully understand them. It means a community acknowledging the wrong that has been done, even if (in fact, especially where) the community itself is implicated in the wrongdoing.

Those who have suffered trauma through abuse "want their communities to recognize their suffering and to acknowledge the seriousness of the harm they have endured. As individuals they want the people who form their moral communities to hear them, to believe them, to recognize that they have been hurt, and to offer help and support."[45]

When a community acknowledges the things that have happened, the sense of isolation changes. The person is no longer alone with their suffering; they now have a

---

45 Judith Herman, *Truth and Repair: How Trauma Survivors Envision Justice* (Basic Books, 2023), p. 81-82.

community who sees and understands their pain. Of course, tacit acknowledgement will not suffice. It takes time to truly understand what has happened and the way that it has impacted the person concerned. A community needs to give sufficient time to listening.

The classic outline of recovery from trauma describes three steps: first, establishing safety; second, remembering and grieving; third, reconnecting again with ordinary life.[46] When a community starts to listen to a person's suffering and shows that it wants to understand that suffering, that person begins to believe that this community could become a safe place for them. The establishment of safety does not, of course, happen overnight. A community, by definition, is a collection of individuals, and they may speak with different voices. The ability to trust in a community develops slowly.

A person who has experienced harm, and especially harm in the context of church, has good reasons to be cautious of the care they will receive from church. Venturing back into a church community will require courage and can be helped by knowing that specified individuals are aware just how demanding the process may be. One person I know who embarked on that process wanted to know that there were several individuals in the church who knew the struggle they were facing. They did not need those individuals to come and speak with them each time they were at church; knowing that they were aware of the situation and ready to support if needed was enough. Making this "refuge" available provided some tangible evidence that this community could be trusted.

---

46 *Trauma and Recovery*, p. 155.

Gospel-shaped relationships in the context of trauma

Many of the ways a community can support (or fail to support) someone who has suffered trauma are widely applicable; they are relevant to every community. However, there are some aspects of a Christian community that are uniquely relevant to the care of a person who has suffered from trauma. We will look at some of the practical implications in the next chapter, but first I want to identify three broad gospel themes and show how they are connected to the care of individuals who have experienced the impact of trauma. It is vital to appreciate that these truths need to be *experienced*. It is not enough to tell a person impacted by trauma that certain things are true. They need to experience these truths as they are lived out within the body of Christ.

1. Identity

Those who have faced trauma often experience a disturbance of their sense of self. A new vulnerability may have arrived. They may feel less valuable. After trauma, there are often feelings of guilt (whether justified or not): "Why didn't I see this coming?" "How could I have been so stupid?" "I could have done more to stop this." Such feelings can leave a person thinking of themselves as weak or useless or simply inferior to others who, they imagine, would have responded better.

A Christian understanding of identity is rooted in grace. A believer is made new in Christ: "Therefore, if anyone is in Christ, the new creation has come: the old has gone, the new is here!" (2 Corinthians 5:17); "I have been crucified with Christ and I no longer live, but Christ lives in me" (Galatians 2:20). This new identity is given, not earned. This is our identity in Christ, and it comes to us as gift; and nothing that we do, nor anything that is done to us, can erode or erase it.

A Christian community will want not only teach to this truth but to live it out in the unity they experience as brothers and sisters in Christ. Such a community is based not on merit or performance but on the gracious gift granted equally to each one. Such a community experience can speak with enormous power to those who, through trauma, have come to believe themselves less worthy, less loved and less lovable. Instead of feelings of shame, they are reminded of the dignity given to them because of their new status in Christ: "See what great love the Father has lavished on us, that we should be called children of God!" (1 John 3:1).

2. Acceptance

Closely tied to the issue of identity is the experience of acceptance. Instead of isolation, believers are reminded that they belong to the body of Christ. In that body each part recognises the suffering of the others: "Its parts should have equal concern for each other. If one part suffers, every part suffers with it" (1 Corinthians 12:25-26).

A church family can, simply through its reliability, become a safe place for someone who has faced trauma. When a community comes to embody towards one another the grace they have themselves experienced in Christ, that community will communicate acceptance and safety. In that context, a person who has experienced trauma can speak of what they have experienced and find that, instead of being met with rejection or blame, they continue to be accepted and welcomed.

Serene Jones is an American theologian and academic. In her book *Trauma and Grace*, she includes a chapter about her use of a commentary on the Psalms that was written by the 16th-century Protestant Reformer John Calvin. She notes how "throughout the commentary, Calvin uses the language of testifying and witnessing to describe what happens when a person turns to God in prayer".[47] She connects this to the experience of trauma survivors and the importance they attach to being heard and accepted.

In testifying, the survivor gives voice to previously unspeakable agony, and in witnessing, the receiver of the testimony is able to confirm that the survivor's voice is heard and that the plight no longer needs to be hidden in a dark corner of the soul, but can be pulled into the light of day and affirmed as a reality worthy of sustained lamentation and possible redress.[48]

We will think more about this process when we consider the place of lament in chapter 12.

3. Involvement

In Ephesians 4, having emphasised the unity of the body of Christ, Paul goes on to say, "to each one of us grace has been given as Christ apportioned it" (Ephesians 4:7). It soon becomes clear that this grace is given to "equip [God's] people for works of service, so that the body of Christ may be built up" (v 12). A person who has endured trauma can feel worthless and as if they have nothing to offer. This sets them apart from the wider community, their inability only reinforcing their sense of alienation and difference.

Yet the New Testament speaks consistently about the way every part of the body of Christ is needed and every member has a part to play. "The whole body ... grows and builds itself up in love, as each part does its work" (v 16). Paul famously tells the church in Corinth that "the eye cannot say to the hand, 'I don't need you!' And the head cannot say to the feet, 'I don't need you!' On the contrary, those parts of

---

47 *Trauma and Grace* (Westminster John Knox Press, 2019), p. 54. While not agreeing with all of Jones' theological convictions, I have found her reflections on theology and trauma to include many helpful and insightful observations.
48 As above, p. 54.

the body that seem to be weaker are indispensable, and the parts that we think are less honourable we treat with special honour" (1 Corinthians 12: 21-23).

Trauma can lead people to doubt their ability to be an active and engaged participant in relationships. They imagine they have nothing constructive to offer because what has happened to them has left them struggling to believe they belong or have any value or can make any contribution in serving others. This emphasis—that, within the body of Christ, every person has a role to play—can be of enormous significance in helping to restore a sense of relational agency. Grace gives value and dignity to the varied gifts and strengths of each person. In this context, they can discover, or rediscover, their place as a valued and necessary member of the community.

The suffering they have endured may even become the basis of the contribution they make. As a person discovers how God meets them with compassion and mercy, those same qualities of compassion and mercy begin to be embodied in their relationship with others. They discover the truth of Paul's words at the start of his second letter to the Corinthians: "Praise be to the God and Father of our Lord Jesus Christ, the Father of compassion and the God of all comfort, who comforts us in all our troubles, *so that we can comfort those in any trouble with the comfort we ourselves receive from God*" (2 Corinthians 1:3-4, emphasis added). That the experience of suffering could be anything other than a source of damage and pain is a possibility many trauma sufferers will never have previously entertained. But the Christian faith places Christ's own suffering at the very centre of its reality. Christians, above all others, have reasons to speak redemptively about suffering. For a person for whom suffering has only ever seemed to be a source of shame and hurt, the possibility that it might, in some way, be enabling and could even bring hope is radically powerful.

Questions for reflection

1. Even where your experiences have not involved severe suffering, can you recall times when an experience of hardship has left you feeling isolated from others in your church family?

2. What factors do you think are most likely to prevent a church from reaching out to and including someone who has undergone a trauma experience?

3. Shame is a key part of the relational damage that trauma can cause. Why should a Christian community be particularly good at dealing with the experience of shame?

SECTION 3

RESPONDING WITH COMPASSION IN THE LOCAL CHURCH

SECTION 3

INTRODUCTION

Many Christians and churches know they are unfamiliar with the way trauma can impact an individual, and they want to be better informed. But this is not just an academic interest—we want to be better *equipped* in order to welcome and support those who are struggling. Trauma disrupts relationships and often produces a sense of isolation. Churches want to be places where connections—both with Christ and with others—can flourish.

This book is not intended to be a trauma-recovery guide. Nor is it designed to equip people for any kind of trauma counselling. Some Christians will want to develop the experience and skill to engage in care at that level, but for most of us, our ambitions will be much more modest. We simply want to better understand people who have experienced trauma so that we can be good friends and can provide wise pastoral care. We want to know how to speak wisely and avoid clumsy missteps.

The chapters in this section of the book provide pointers to what those wise and godly conversations might look like. They seek to help us overcome feelings of inadequacy and ignorance that can leave us fearful of saying anything at all. They also seek to help us know our limits.

When a person arrives at our church, we will not, generally, know anything about them. Trauma may have been part of their life experience. It may still be affecting them in the present. But we will not know that. And it is unlikely to be one of the first things we discover about them.

Chapter 10 therefore provides some commonsense principles to help ensure that our initial welcome is sensitive to that possibility.

If people do choose to share difficult experiences from their past and how those experiences continue to affect them, they may or may not use the language of trauma. Chapter 11 provides some initial thoughts about how we can respond in ways that are wise and kind rather than thoughtless and clumsy.

Chapters 12–14 offer further pointers to the way the gospel of Jesus Christ speaks into the experience of trauma. These reflections are not a template for a trauma-recovery programme nor guidance notes for some kind of trauma counselling. They simply provide reflections on ways that the grace of Christ can speak into the struggles that people affected by trauma typically experience, to help you as you seek to support others—or, indeed, in your own experience of trauma.

CHAPTER 10

A THOUGHTFUL WELCOME

Churches work hard at welcoming people—or they should do! They appoint welcome teams and welcome co-ordinators. They set out welcome desks and serve welcome suppers. They sense, rightly, that the gracious welcome we have received from Christ should be echoed in the welcome we extend to others (Romans 15:7). "Do not forget to show hospitality to strangers, for by so doing some people have shown hospitality to angels without knowing it" (Hebrews 13:2).

But what if our lack of familiarity with "strangers" involves something more significant than being unaware of a person's name? Chapter 3 introduced us to Naomi and the email she sent to a church office:

The email that arrived in the church office was distinctly unusual. Aisha, who worked there part-time, read it twice but still couldn't quite make sense of it. It seemed so odd that she wondered if she should simply delete it. But eventually she decided to mention it to the pastor. The email was asking about arranging a meeting with someone from the church—but gave no details about why a meeting was wanted or what the meeting would be about. The person writing also said they would like to choose who they met with and asked if they could have a list of options. What seemed to Aisha as particularly odd was that the email stipulated that the meeting had to take place away from the

*church building. It was all so very demanding, and
it really didn't help that the tone of the email was so
abrupt. The pastor checked the name of the sender but
didn't recognise it. He said it was definitely odd and
that he'd think about it before replying. That was more
than a week ago now. Aisha suspected he had probably
forgotten. She couldn't decide whether to remind him or
simply delete the email and forget it.*

Naomi had sent the email because, although she desperately
wanted to be involved with church, a long period of abuse
at the hands of a church pastor meant she was profoundly
anxious and fearful about doing so.

Naomi's experience had left her with what could reasonably be described as a kind of vulnerability or weakness
in relation to church. In a different context, the New Testament encourages the "strong" to bear generously with
those who are "weak" (Romans 15:1). In his parable looking towards his return, Jesus commends the "sheep on his
right" who have invited the stranger in, clothed the naked
and looked after those who were ill. By contrast, he con-
demns the "goats on his left", who have not done these
things (Matthew 25:31-46).

A victim of church abuse once commented to me that it
can sometimes seem as if our safeguarding procedures are
better at mobilising support for perpetrators than they are
for victims. When someone arrives at a church and presents a safeguarding concern, a safeguarding plan is put in
place. An accountability group is created, and the perpetrator is linked with a group of wise and thoughtful church
members. That group will meet with them regularly to
offer support. Yet our churches are much less likely to have
clear procedures in place for those who have been victims
of trauma. A church may be alert to safeguarding issues

but what provision will they put in place for those who, like Naomi, have suffered trauma? Can she expect that a supportive group of wise and thoughtful church members will be created around her?

What, then, might a thoughtful welcome for Naomi look like? Here are three elements to consider.

1. A general awareness of the category of trauma

A church is more likely to care well for someone like Naomi if they have a basic awareness of trauma and the various ways it can impact a person. It is particularly important that the leadership of a church—and especially the pastoral staff— are alert to the category of trauma. They are often the first people to engage in depth with those new to a church, and if they have the category of trauma in mind, this increases the likelihood that they will respond well.

As Naomi's story makes clear, however, this awareness needs to extend more widely. The administrative staff who received Naomi's email in the church office thought that what she wrote was "odd" and "demanding"—that she was being difficult. It appears that the pastor felt similarly. They saw Naomi as someone who was being problematic and un-reasonable, which meant that whatever response they made (if they responded at all) was always likely to have a reluc-tant and grudging feel to it.

However much we might wish it were otherwise, people arriving at a church for the first time do often find it diffi-cult and threatening. This is more so for someone who isn't a Christian and more so again for someone who has expe-rienced trauma. Recognising this is important. A different perspective on the part of the office staff and pastor would have led to a very different response to Naomi's email; what if their minds had considered the possibility that the email was sent by someone who had suffered badly—who had been badly sinned against? That would have shaped a very different attitude and consequently a very different response.

Every church member is called to bring an attitude of grace towards those who, for whatever reason, find themselves on the margins. The way a church responds to those who struggle to fit in is one measure of the extent to which a gospel culture has been established. Christ went to the outcast and the marginalised (Luke 5:30-32). God "chose the lowly things of this world and the despised things— and the things that are not" (1 Corinthians 1:28). A church that is alert to the category of trauma and the way it can disrupt relationships will be more able to reflect this culture of grace.

As well as a general awareness of trauma, there are some more specific ways a church can respond well.

2. A responsiveness to less common behaviours and requests

Someone affected by trauma will often find fitting in with the normal conventions of church difficult. As one writer puts it, "Consider how it must feel constantly to experience all new experiences as though being under threat".[49] Realising that some people do experience new situations in this way will help us understand how even unexceptional aspects of church can become incredibly demanding and difficult situations to navigate.

Arriving at a church building may be hard, particularly if that involves passing through a crowded entrance area. Entering through a quieter side door might be helpful. However, if that door isn't usually available for access and it needs

---

49 Joanna Naomi Douglas, *Building a Trauma-Informed Worshipping Community*, p. 20.

unlocking each Sunday, the church must both understand the need for flexibility and be ready to show it.

Someone might ask to sit in a quiet room away from the main church gathering or step outside the building altogether in order to avoid the noise and pressure of the main body of the church. If we don't appreciate why a person might request this provision, churches may simply see this as something contrary to their desire for the unity of the church. In emphasising the importance of gathering with the rest of the church body, they may resist the request.

Those affected by trauma often have heightened levels of arousal, and this can make them feel trapped when they are in a busy building. They may want to sit at the back or in a seat close to an exit. They may want a clear view of the exit and find it difficult if people stand or sit in front of the exit door. These preferences mean a person may well make requests that seem odd or difficult. Realising that such requests might be prompted by past experiences of severe suffering will help a church respond graciously and generously.

A welcome team who are comfortable with people coming in and out during a church service is very different to one who communicate disapproval of what they see as disruptive behaviour. If a church makes clear that they are comfortable with unusual or atypical behaviour, this may help someone struggling with the idea of coming into church to at least make the attempt.

Given care and support, such struggles might lessen so that a person no longer experiences the same difficulties when they are part of a church gathering or in a midweek group. But working toward that change takes time. It will take time for that person to speak about their struggles in the first place. A trusting relationship is needed before someone will feel safe enough to explain their difficulties. We

have to learn to be patient—the first characteristic of love
(1 Corinthians 13:4).

3. Preachers who are alert to the impact their words may have

Preachers cannot know, never mind make allowances for,
the circumstances of all the people to whom they preach.
In conversation, we can choose our words and tone of voice
and illustrations according to the person in front of us.
Some of that happens instinctively based on the feedback
we are getting in a conversation. In preaching, that simply
is not possible. Preachers do get feedback from a congregation, but it is not individual. Even if they did know every
detail of every person before them and could absorb every
person's individual feedback, there still wouldn't be a happy
"middle path" which made allowance for each one. Preachers whose prime ambition is to keep everyone happy will
not be preachers who are faithful to God and his word.

But preaching that is driven by people-pleasing is not at
all the same thing as preaching that is determined to care
for the weak and vulnerable. Matthew identifies many Old
Testament prophecies that are fulfilled in Christ. One identifies Jesus as the Servant promised in Isaiah and declares
that he is the one of whom it is said, "A bruised reed he will
not break, and a smouldering wick he will not snuff out"
(Matthew 12:20, quoting Isaiah 42:3). Those experiencing
the aftermath of severe suffering can certainly be considered
as bruised reeds, fragile and easily broken. How might a
preacher reflect this kind of Christ-like care? Here are some
suggestions.

1. A preacher will begin by assuming that someone with
   an experience of severe suffering may well be present
   when they preach.

2. A preacher will want to identify aspects of their sermon that may be difficult for some people. A passage might, for example, refer to suffering in conceptual terms. But for someone whose experience of suffering continues to affect them daily, speaking of suffering in abstract terms will sit uneasily. For them, the impact of suffering is anything but abstract. A brief comment which recognises that some will have that perspective may be all that is needed. Trauma leaves a person feeling alienated and relationally detached—"No one understands what I have been through". A brief comment may be enough to challenge that belief and give a sense that this church might be one that will notice them.

3. Sometimes a preacher will speak from a passage that addresses suffering head-on. Many psalms do this in general terms, which means we can "borrow" the psalmists' words for our own specific struggles. Narrative passages relate specific suffering. Examples, many of which we've already noticed, include the bereavements and losses recorded in the book of Ruth; the multiple losses and abuse faced by another Tamar in Genesis 38; many passages that record sexually abusive behaviour (for example Genesis 19; Genesis 39; 2 Samuel 11 and 13); passages detailing physical brutality (for example Judges 21) and passages describing warfare and sieges (for example 2 Kings 6 and 25).

These passages will land in a particular way with those who have suffered significant trauma. When a Bible reading and sermon are going to be grappling with a difficult topic or incident, it would be good to make this clear at the start of a church service. This may help someone who has suffered trauma to feel noticed. It may be appropriate to acknowledge that some may not feel ready to engage with a particular reading and may want to step out. Providing this option is an even stronger way of making those who have suffered trauma feel noticed and safe. Trauma often involves the loss of agency and choice, and taking this approach can help avoid revisiting a similar loss of control in the present.

4. There are also implications for the content of a sermon. When preaching from passages that describe severe suffering, preachers may be tempted to try and lighten the mood with a witty comment. However, remarks that seem witty to the preacher can sound like an insensitive trivialising of suffering and pain. When preaching on accounts of abuse or brutality, it will help simply to acknowledge the unpleasant nature of an account. This doesn't mean apologising for the passage or seeming to suggest it shouldn't be in Scripture. It simply recognises that anyone who allows their heart to really enter into the incident being described will find it hard. Such an acknowledgement both notices and expresses concern for those who are affected by a past experience of suffering, and it reminds those who are not that there may be others around them who are affected and who need care (or, at the very least, prayer). This can help a person to feel affirmed as a part of a church family rather than alienated from it.

Essentials of church life

It is not possible to make allowances for every different preference and perspective that exists within a church family. But there is a strong argument for making provision for those whose lives have been impacted by some kind of extreme suffering. A readiness (or, better, an eagerness) to care for those experiencing suffering should be a central feature of a Christian community. Jesus moved in compassion toward those who suffered. The church in Acts responded with material generosity to anyone who had need (Acts 2:45). Paul likens his ministry to that of a nursing mother caring for her children (1 Thessalonians 2:7-8).

Fostering a gospel culture therefore looks like wanting to recognise those in our churches whose experience of extreme suffering continues to trouble them in the present; wanting to think hard about how to provide a welcome and a ministry that loves them and cares well for them.

It also looks like wanting to pray. One of the distinctive features of God's people must be an eagerness to bring before God the needs of those who struggle. Prayerfully seeking help when we find ourselves faced with difficulties that seem beyond us is the right and proper thing to do.

A note about the language of "trauma informed"

"Are you trauma informed?" is an increasingly common question and may well be asked of a church. It's not a phrase that everyone feels comfortable with. To some, declaring yourself to be a "trauma-informed church" or promising to offer "trauma-informed counselling" feels problematic. Darby Strickland comments helpfully in this way:

> "When I first heard the term trauma informed, I thought, 'Why would I want trauma to inform my care? I want the Bible to inform my care!' And rightly so. We need to be on guard against taking on a world view that is centered around trauma ... Scripture's perspectives on human suffering, sin, and redemption should control how we understand traumatic experiences and approach survivors.

> *"At the same time, there is tremendous value in being trauma informed—in reading widely to understand the impacts and effects of trauma on a person. Literature on trauma encapsulates key research and a wealth of case studies that help us to see impacts of trauma that are not immediately apparent."*[50]

If being better informed about the different ways trauma can impact a person enables us to seek out the resources of Scripture more fully and more faithfully, then being trauma informed will be a good thing. If it takes us away from Scripture and forms in us a mindset that limits or eclipses the Spirit's work in a person's life, then it is problematic. Whether we use the term "trauma informed" or whether we prefer not to is much less important than whether we accurately understand the experience of those who have faced severe suffering and whether we determine to find ways to offer them biblically wise love and care.

Questions for reflection

1. Why do you think we can sometimes respond negatively to unusual requests?
2. If you have a church building, do you think any of its features might be difficult for someone for whom coming into church is difficult? Can any of those features be changed?
3. What steps could you take to make your church more alert to the difficulties experienced by someone who has experienced severe suffering?

---

50 *Trauma: Caring for Survivors*, p. 4-5.

CHAPTER 11

CONVERSATIONS ABOUT TRAUMA

There are two kinds of mistake churches can make in responding to those affected by trauma. The first is to find the whole area so confusing and troubling that they do nothing. It is easy to end up seeing the care of those affected by trauma as "specialist territory" which must only be attempted by experts. Over-fearful of getting it wrong and doing harm, such churches adopt a hands-off attitude. But this can leave people who have experienced trauma feeling both ignored and neglected. Moreover, given the widespread experience of trauma and the limited availability of specialist care, many of those affected will not have access to experts. So, even though as Christians we must certainly know our limits, there will always be things that we can do. We shouldn't do nothing.

The second mistake is to believe ourselves capable of doing anything and everything that might be needed to care for someone with trauma. Such a church has an exaggerated and misplaced confidence in their own capacity. Perhaps it is expressed in terms of confidence in the sufficiency of Scripture but without acknowledging limitations in our ability to handle Scripture wisely in every context. Usually this confidence arises because of a naivety about the kinds of difficulties trauma can produce and a gross simplification about what is needed in the process of recovery. It is vital that a church should recognise its limits and not assume that knowing the gospel and having God's word means it can or must simply try to do everything.

A word about spectrums

We have seen how the impact of trauma can vary widely from person to person. This means that what a person might need in the aftermath of trauma will also vary widely. It would be a mistake to think in terms of simple categories. People differ—both those affected by trauma and those who seek to help them. It is helpful to think in terms of four spectrums.

1. Severity of impact

The severity of the *event* a person has experienced is, as we've seen, not a reliable guide to the impact it may have. One person may have been caught up in an appalling natural disaster or war zone and have seen many die in terrible circumstances; another may have witnessed a relatively minor road traffic accident in which only limited injuries were sustained. Yet it could still be the observer of the accident who is most affected by trauma. An important spectrum, then, concerns the extent of the *impact* on a person. The frequency and intensity of flashbacks; the level of hyperarousal; the degree of disturbed mood; the extent of interference with normal life; the presence or absence of disassociation—these will all be measures of the severity of the impact that trauma has had on a person. Rather than communicate our assessment of what we consider an appropriate response to a particular event, we should simply notice what is there.

2. Complexity of the trauma

Sometimes trauma arises in the context of a single event. But it can also arise as a result of extended periods of suffering.

"Complex trauma" is the phrase commonly used to describe such situations, and even though there has been some debate about the term, certain experiences of trauma are clearly complicated. Protracted suffering, especially when it is experienced in the context of family, will often have a complex impact on a person's life and wellbeing. The earlier that trauma happens, the more complicated that impact tends to be.

3. Experience in relation to trauma

Turning to those who are seeking to come alongside those struggling with trauma, people have different levels of familiarity with trauma. This is true both for those in our church communities and those in the caring professions. Partly this is dependent on the extent of reading and thinking a person has done, but still more it will be affected by the time they have spent supporting those whose lives have been affected by trauma. It is also worth saying that we all have different ways of responding to, and different capacities in shouldering, what is shared with us or asked of us.

4. Role of those offering support

A person offering help may have one of many different roles. Consider even this limited list:

- Pre-existing close friend
- Pre-existing relationship, but not close
- A new friend and supporter
- Pastor/elder
- Small-group leader
- Pastoral carer
- Informal lay counsellor
- Formal counsellor
- Trauma therapist

The responsibilities and expectations associated with each of these roles vary considerably, and there will be variation within each of these categories as well.

Seven pointers for beneficial conversations

So, as we spend the rest of the chapter thinking about what is involved in having wise and loving conversations with those whose lives have been affected by trauma, we need to remember these spectrums, because they will have a bearing on the kind of support and therefore the kinds of conversations that will be appropriate. What will be wise in one situation will be foolish in another. What one person badly wants will feel like an unwanted intrusion to another. It's not easy. Thankfully, we have a God who gives wisdom to those who know they lack it and who ask him for his help (James 1:5).

In what follows, the sufferers I have in mind are not those who have in the past faced the most severe and complex experiences of trauma. Nor do I have in mind those who, in the present, are experiencing effects that are particularly intense. Helping people manage such experiences is not the focus for this chapter.

With those caveats in place, then, here are seven pointers for conversations with those affected by trauma

1. Talk about talking

Whenever we are giving support to another person, it is always important to be clear about what is and is not wanted. It is also important to be clear about what is and is not being offered. It is so very easy to make wrong assumptions. We might assume that a person wants to describe the trauma they have faced—or that they don't. A conversation about what is wanted will help to clarify that. "Is the accident something that you do want to talk about at some point?" "Does it help to talk about what happened? Or is it too difficult to do that?" "I realise you may not want to, or even be allowed to, talk about what happened while you were in the army, but what would be helpful?"

Talking about talking is one part of building a trusting relationship. It can be important to demonstrate that, on the one hand, you are not frightened of talking about a person's trauma but that equally, you are not going to pressure them to talk. Talking about talking helps reassure a person that you will be a considerate and careful conversation partner.

Of course, even when someone tells us what it is they want, it doesn't follow that we are the right person to meet that need. At any point, we may come to realise that we lack either the skill or experience to provide the support that is needed. That doesn't mean that we withdraw our support. It means that part of our talking about talking may lead us to explore with the person whether there is someone else who could be involved—someone else who brings more expertise and/or experience and who can, therefore, offer things that we can't.

2. Notice ongoing issues

Sometimes trauma doesn't simply concern an event in the past. Sometimes trauma is a present and ongoing experience. We might think of a situation where a person is facing chronic illness or is supporting someone close to them through a period of severe illness; or one involving ongoing abuse. Assessing and, wherever possible, establishing a person's safety is a first priority. Just what is required in such situations will vary hugely, but it includes the involvement of external agencies who have the necessary experience and safeguarding skills, particularly where there are concerns about domestic abuse.

3. Get an overview of their experience of trauma

Where a person does want to talk about their trauma, it usually makes sense to get a broad outline of what has happened. This is different to obtaining a detailed account of what has taken place. Revisiting an experience of trauma is not straightforward. As we've seen, when a person recounts what happened, it often feels more like reliving the trauma. Initially, therefore, we will simply want a basic outline of what has happened. As we invite this broadbrush account, we should avoid questions about details. Such questions are likely evoke flashback experiences. A wise question would be something simply like "Do you feel able to give me just a broad picture of what it is that happened?"

This overview will also mean getting an impression of the present-day impact of the trauma. We may want to ask if there has been any impact on sleep or work life. Trauma is often experienced at a bodily level, and asking about physical symptoms can be important. Similarly, asking about any disruption to relationships and everyday functioning will help us understand the severity of the struggles. Open questions allow a person to answer with as much or as little detail as they wish: "How do you sense all this is affecting you now?" "What's hardest about all this in the present?"

In the context of church, specific but not leading questions about spiritual wellbeing will usually be appropriate. "How has this affected your faith?" "What has this meant for your relationship with the Lord?" "Are you still able to pray or is that difficult now?" Experiencing trauma can bring about a crisis of faith, and it is important to be alert to that possibility. "Has this left you with any new questions about God or any new doubts that you didn't have before?"

It is important to establish, again at a broad level, the kind of emotional impact that trauma has had. Lowered mood and increased anxiety are common, and an assessment of the risk of self-harm may be needed. (Again, most Christians will need to seek advice if they are concerned about this in any way.)

4. Consider whether others should be involved

From the very outset, it is important to keep asking ourselves whether there are others who should be involved in providing support. Anyone offering support must always be alert to the possibility that they are getting out of their depth and be ready to discuss additional options. This would not mean withdrawing support—it's not helpful to think of this in terms of "referring someone on". Rather, it means talking with someone about their various options and working with them to decide whether additional support should be sought and, if so, from where.

Involving a family doctor may be an important step, especially where there are prominent physical symptoms, so that the possibility of underlying medical problems can be considered.

5. Listen and witness

Listening and understanding is vital in supporting someone who has experienced trauma. This needs saying because when we see someone struggling because of what they have suffered, we naturally want to make things better. Something in us rightly wants to take away their pain. But if this leads us to start offering "solutions", we are likely to misstep. Perhaps we might start urging various actions or activities. Or we may offer a whole range of Bible verses that we think provide the answers which that person needs in order to "accept" their experience. But simple and quick solutions for trauma are rarely available. What is often most important to those affected by trauma is that someone might listen carefully to them and really begin to understand what they have been through. This process takes time and, initially at least, may not seem to be making any difference. Yet this "witnessing" function is crucial. It helps to overcome the sense of relational isolation that so often accompanies an experience of trauma. It makes such a difference when someone else is willing to hear what has happened and is ready to stand with that person and feel something of the awfulness of their experience.

Something very significant happens when a story is witnessed and heard, perhaps for the very first time. It reflects enormous courage on the part of the victim of trauma, it represents a willingness for them to trust, and it offers an opportunity to be known and understood. It can give them a sense of value and dignity. It also builds a relationship in which another is coming alongside so that, insofar as they are able, they can help to carry the burden.

6. Expand church connections

It is important to work out which other people are or could be involved in providing support. In some cases, we may be the only person who has listened to a person's struggle. A key part of our role, however, will probably be making sure that we don't remain the only person who has listened. Helping others to be involved—especially others in the church—is a further step in overcoming the relational isolation that trauma brings.

In practical terms, this may involve nothing more complicated than introducing them to others in the church family. With permission, this might include giving others some background information about the struggles a person has faced and even some brief guidelines about what will and won't be helpful.

It may also involve helping a person integrate into a pastoral group in the church. Attending a small group can be an incredibly difficult prospect and may need thinking through at length before it can become a possibility. Establishing what can be said to the group leaders will be important. You may decide to offer to join the person in meeting the group leaders and using that meeting to give some agreed information about the trauma and its impact.

7. Involve a person in church life
Experiences of trauma often significantly disturb a person's involvement in everyday life. The impact on a person's sense of self may mean that roles and responsibilities which were once commonplace now seem impossible. Helping them restore aspects of themselves that have been disrupted is an important element in recovery. But these things cannot be rushed, and a readiness to be involved will often fluctuate considerably. At the right time, however, we may want to help a person find areas of service in the church. Doing so in the context of a gracious and patient church, where weaknesses and failings are managed well, is usually a great blessing.

Questions for reflection
1. In which direction are you most likely to veer: toward avoiding conversations about trauma or to an over-confidence in this area?
2. If you did feel out of your depth in these kinds of conversations, where could you seek help?
3. Why do you think witnessing is so important? Why does it often matter so much to people who have experienced trauma that they be heard and understood?

CHAPTER 12

TRAUMA AND LAMENT

Until relatively recently, the biblical practice of lament has been notable by its absence from the lives both of most Christians and most churches. It simply has not featured.

In his book *Dark Clouds, Deep Mercy*, Mark Vroegop emphasises how costly this oversight has been:

> *"Lament is how we bring our sorrow to God. Without lament we won't know how to process pain. Silence, bitterness, and even anger can dominate our spiritual lives instead ... Lament is how Christians grieve. It is how to help hurting people. Lament is how we learn important truths about God and our world ... we need to recover the ancient practice of lament and the grace that comes through it. Christianity suffers when lament is missing."* [51]

The relevance of the practice of lament to the experience of trauma is obvious. Lament allows a person to do two critical things: to express the pain and bewilderment of suffering, and to do so in a way that maintains an orientation toward God. Lament has been described as "the honest cry of a hurting heart wrestling with the paradox of pain and the promise of God's goodness".[52] This capacity to express pain in God's presence without abandoning trust in his goodness is critical.

---

51 *Dark Clouds, Deep Mercy: Discovering the Grace of Lament* (Crossway, 2019), p. 21.
52 As above, p. 26.

When trauma raises questions about the goodness of God, lament helps a person wrestle with two realities. On the one hand there is their experience of suffering—something terrible has happened to them. On the other hand, there is goodness—both the goodness that still exists in the world and, still more importantly, the goodness of God. For a believer to find a way through trauma means finding a way to hold both of these realities without minimising either of them.

As we've seen, a key problem in trauma is the lack of words. When something is "unspeakably awful", an absence of words interferes with our attempts to tell the story of our life. We use stories to explain ourselves to others and, perhaps even more importantly, to make sense of ourselves. Without words there are no stories. This means that those struggling with trauma can find it almost impossible to integrate what has happened to them.

The lament psalms provide words. These words express pain and struggle in general terms—the particular peril or disaster that prompted the words of lament is rarely made clear. This makes the psalms of lament adaptable: they can be used by people whose suffering has happened in all manner of different contexts.

Mark Vroegop's book sets out a framework that has helped many engage with the psalms of lament for the first time. It involves four stages: turn, complain, ask and trust. That framework can help us apply the practice of lament in the context of trauma.

1. Turn

For many who have been affected by trauma, turning to God simply doesn't seem possible. What has happened is too awful, too incoherent, too overwhelming for them to bring it to anyone, and that includes God. Anger and bewilderment may be prominent emotions for those who have suffered trauma. But can these things be spoken of to God? It often isn't clear what prayer about trauma would look like. What exactly would they be asking for? The traumatic event has happened. There is no point in asking God to take it away.

As well as struggling to articulate what has happened, people may also struggle to describe the impact of the trauma. All of this makes it very hard to know what it is that they are asking God to do.

The psalms of lament give some astonishing and heart-wrenching words. Consider this from Psalm 88, the deepest and darkest of all the laments:

"I am overwhelmed with troubles
and my life draws near to death.
I am counted among those who go down to the pit;
I am like one without strength.
I am set apart with the dead,
like the slain who lie in the grave,
whom you remember no more,
who are cut off from your care.

"You have put me in the lowest pit,
in the darkest depths.
Your wrath lies heavily on me;
you have overwhelmed me with all your waves.
You have taken from me my closest friends
and have made me repulsive to them.
I am confined and cannot escape;
my eyes are dim with grief.

"I call to you, LORD, every day;
I spread out my hands to you.
Do you show your wonders to the dead?
Do their spirits rise up and praise you?
Is your love declared in the grave,

your faithfulness in Destruction?
Are your wonders known in the place of darkness,
or your righteous deeds in the land of oblivion?

"But I cry to you for help, LORD;
in the morning my prayer comes before you.
Why, LORD, do you reject me
and hide your face from me?

"From my youth I have suffered and been close to death;
I have borne your terrors and am in despair.
Your wrath has swept over me;
your terrors have destroyed me.
All day long they surround me like a flood;
they have completely engulfed me.
You have taken from me friend and neighbour—
darkness is my closest friend." (Psalm 88:3-18)

The psalm's images express the experience of harm: there is a pit, there are dark depths, overwhelming waves, darkness, terrors, the surrounding of a flood and the sense of being engulfed. The psalm also captures a whole range of emotions: despair, anger, bewilderment, humiliation.

Typically, a psalm of lament begins in struggle and complaint before moving on to hope and trust. But in Psalm 88, there is no transition. The psalm ends in despair. Why would God choose to include a psalm like this in the Bible? The answer, it seems, is because these words of complaint and despair are, despite their desperate tone, still spoken to someone. They are, therefore, words of faith—the psalmist still believes there is a God to complain to.

We should not underestimate how important it is for a person who has experienced trauma to take this step. Turning to God in this way doesn't solve anything. It doesn't resolve the pain or answer every question, but it is a beginning.

It removes the sense of isolation. They have someone to speak to. And it is understandable if those words, at least at first, are simply words of complaint.

2. Complaint

The language of complaint is prominent in most of the lament psalms. Often this is couched in terms of questions.

"Why, LORD, do you stand far off? Why do you hide yourself in times of trouble?" (Psalm 10:1)

"O God, why have you rejected us for ever? Why does your anger smoulder against the sheep of your pasture?" (Psalm 74:1)

"How can we sing the songs of the LORD while in a foreign land?" (Psalm 137:4)

The psalmist expresses bewilderment: *I don't get it. I don't understand. Why would you allow this? Why didn't you do something? Why do these things just go on and on with no relief? Is my life going to be dominated by this for ever? How long will it be like this?*

By speaking in this way, the psalmist resists a stoicism which refuses to acknowledge pain; but he also determines not to remain in a state of unresolved, or even unacknowledged, bitterness. Giving voice to complaints means putting into words the horrors of what has happened and everything that is still being felt as a result.

This is a vital step in the process of spiritual recovery. "Complaint is a turning point of lament. Be honest. Talk to God about your struggles. Even if it's messy or embarrassing let biblical complaint push you toward what comes next: asking God for help."[53]

---

53 As above, p. 54.

3. Ask

The danger of putting these four steps into one short chapter is that it risks giving an artificial sense of ease and speed. Wrestling with the experience of severe suffering is neither easy nor speedy. Yet, because we hate to see a person struggling with so much pain, we can want both of these. This means that when we walk alongside those who have suffered trauma, we can be tempted to hurry a person towards a resolution too quickly. But...

> *"A traumatized person should not be expected to speak words of hopefulness or trust in God before he or she is ready. To push somebody too quickly into expressions of positivity and well-being could be the cause of re-traumatization."* [54]

So, while the "pivot" point in the psalms of lament is crucial, we must not arrive at it prematurely. Nevertheless, when a person who has been lost in bewilderment and doubt cautiously begins to speak out their requests, they are beginning to consider the possibility that God might be good after all. They dare to entrust themselves to him. They dare to believe that he will care for them. And they do this even as a part of them is continuing to ask why it seemed that he chose not to care for them in the past:

> *"My God, I cry out by day, but you do not answer, by night, but I find no rest. Yet you are enthroned as the Holy One; you are the one Israel praises." (Psalm 22:2-3)*

"The key word [here]," writes Vroegop, "is *yet*. It becomes a bridge from complaint to bold requests. Don't miss it!"[55]

---

54 Megan Warner, "Bible and Trauma" in Christopher C.H. Cook and Isabelle Hamley (eds), *The Bible and Mental Health: Towards a Biblical Theology of Mental Health* (SCM Press, 2020), p. 202.

55 *Dark Clouds, Deep Mercy*, p. 58.

The nature of those requests will vary, but will often include one or more of the following.

- *Justice:* For some affected by trauma, there will be a sense of injustice, and blame may be felt towards those who contributed to their trauma. In some situations, legal action will be appropriate, but in other circumstances, no human justice can be served. This part of lament may, with the prayers of the psalmists, mean a person entrusting justice to God. As Christopher Ash memorably puts it in his reflections on Romans 12, they must determine to "leave room for an angry God".[56]
- *Security:* In the place of fearful hypervigilance, a person may inch towards a new sense of safety. Many of the psalms give words to a new-found trust that God can keep them safe:

> *"Be my rock of refuge,*
> *to which I can always go;*
> *give the command to save me,*
> *for you are my rock and my fortress."*
> *(Psalm 71:3)*

- *Community:* Those isolated by their past suffering might well want to echo the closing words of Psalm 88—"Darkness is my closest friend". But gradually they may ask God to help them rejoin the community of faith so that they might be able to say, "I will declare your name to my people; in the assembly I will praise you" (Psalm 22:22).
- *Honour:* Shame is prominent in trauma. A person may feel themselves irreparably damaged by what

---

56 Christopher Ash and Steve Midgley, *The Heart of Anger* (Crossway, 2021), p. 101.

has happened. Part of a prayer of lament may involve asking God to restore in them a sense of the worth they have before God: "You will increase my honour and comfort me once more" (Psalm 71:21).

4. Trust

One way to understand the process of recovery from trauma is to see that it involves the long, slow process of arriving at the point where it is possible to know both that terrible evil or suffering has taken place and yet that there is a God who is good. This is so much more than wrestling towards a tentative resolution of the problem of suffering. It is personal. It means finding a way to trust God even in the absence of answers to all our questions.

This journey towards trust is generally slow, but the psalms of lament are excellent travelling companions. "Lament helps us practice active patience. Trust looks like talking to God, sharing our complaints, seeking God's help, and then recommitting ourselves to believe in who God is and what he has done—even as the trial continues. Lament is how we endure. It is how we trust. It is how we wait."[57]

This journey towards trust can be taken either by a whole community or by a single individual. In either case, the communal aspect of lament is important in order that the trauma might be "witnessed". This means that a community both sees what has happened and names it.

Many of the lament psalms end with powerful statements of trust:

"In God I trust and am not afraid. What can man do to me?" (Psalm 56:11)

---

57 *Dark Clouds, Deep Mercy*, p. 74.

*"The LORD is with me; I will not be afraid. What can
mere mortals do to me? The LORD is with me; he is my
helper. I look in triumph on my enemies."*

(Psalm 118:6-7)

The transition from despair to trust is often abrupt. Some
have suggested that it is "the very act of praying the words
of the psalm, before witnesses... [that] causes an emotional shift in the pray-er, so that by the end of the psalm the
person has genuinely moved to a place in which hopefulness,
trust or praise feel right".[58] It would, of course, be a mistake
to urge those who have suffered trauma to speak such words
of trust before they are ready. But when they are ready, the
psalms of lament may prove an invaluable resource in the
long and careful journey of recovery.

Helping others to lament

If you are seeking to walk with someone who is suffering
from trauma, then one way of loving them well and wisely
is to help them to lament. The first and simplest way that
you can do this is just to introduce the possibility. Many
will not have considered lament as something God might
welcome. Or, if they have, they will not have known how
to proceed. You can love someone well by being willing
to spend time with them as you look at a lament psalm
together.

It may well be that you need do little more than invite
someone to read through a psalm of lament and then ask
them what has struck them from the psalm. Is there a particular verse or turn of phrase or idea that resonates with
their own experience? Are there words that capture something that they would want to say to God or say to others? Is

---

58 "Bible and Trauma" in *The Bible and Mental Health*, p. 201.

there a prominent emotion captured in the psalm that they also are feeling?

It is also worth asking yourself whether singing a lament might prove helpful to them. Are there Christian worship songs that they have noticed expressing the pain and struggles they are experiencing? Could they give themselves to singing these words before the Lord?[59]

Some people may be helped by you giving them slightly more structured help. The four categories above provide a framework that may prove helpful. You could invite someone to read a psalm of lament with you and then invite them to pick out phrases that seem to express each of the four elements: turn, complaint, ask, trust. You could then ask them to try to write out their own version of each of these four steps.

- *Turn:* How would they express their own turning towards God as they ask him to meet them in their struggle? What words would they use to declare to God their determination to turn their face towards him?
- *Complaint:* What words of complaint do they want to speak? What is it that feels so wrong? What is it that has so clearly not been as it should be?
- *Ask:* What do they most want from the Lord? How might they start to petition him for blessing and for help?
- *Trust:* What will they try to remember about God's character? How will they express trust in him as a result? What is it that they want to say to express a trusting relationship in the Lord (or, at least, what is it they want to want to say)?

---

59 See Karl Hood, "The Benefits of Singing" in *Journal of Biblical Counseling* 38:2 (2024), p. 75-88.

A process like this will take time. It may mean revisiting the psalm several times—perhaps someone will want to take the psalm away so that they can read and reflect on it during the week before they meet and talk with you a second time. Perhaps they would prefer to write out their words of lament in private and then show them to you only after they have had a chance to consider them on their own.

Lament in a small group

Alternatively (or additionally), some people may find it helpful to use words of lament in the context of a small group. "A number of writers on lament recommend small group practice in particular, suggesting that a small number of group members provides the ideal balance between being witnessed and being able to build and develop strong relationships through the practice."[60] This could be a group of people specifically brought together for the purpose of lamenting. Or it could be a pre-existing small group who offer support to one of their group members.

The format here is likely to be different. It will usually make sense for someone to take the lead in organising the time that the group sets aside to support someone with lament. One person in the group might, initially, read the psalm out loud. Members of the group might each share things that have struck them from the psalm. Where a specific trauma has been experienced by one of the group members, the group leader may want to emphasise that others cannot, of course, understand what that person has gone through. But it may help that person to hear how, in general terms, others in the group notice how both "turning" and "complaining" is captured in the psalm. Hearing, even in very general terms, how others see this expression

---

60 As above.

of the psalmist's experience may prove helpful. As others notice these elements in the psalm, it may seem to grant permission for the person who has suffered trauma to express their own experiences in a way that had not seemed possible before.

Considering a lament in a group like this allows severe suffering to be spoken about. It helps to bring hardship and struggle and wrestling with trust right into the community of faith. It emphasises that these emotions are not only allowed but should be expected in the face of trauma.

A group could end its time by reading the psalm out loud together. It may be important for the group leader to emphasise that while for some the words of the psalm may accurately capture their emotions, that will not be so for everyone. For some the psalm will feel more aspirational. It expresses what they one day hope to be able to say, but they aren't there yet. They are choosing to express their faith by identifying themselves with the words of the psalm and the words that are spoken by the wider Christian community, convinced that these convey truth that they long to own in their experience again,

For some this reading aloud may itself prove to be the single most significant expression of turning and trusting.

Corporate lament

Finally, it is worth thinking about the place of lament in our church services. Lament needs time, and it needs reflection. It involves making space to experience and express strong emotions and feelings. Sadly, many of our church gatherings don't have space for this.

It may require a more specific plan if we are going to include an element of lament. This could take the form of a reading from a psalm, a period of quiet and then a sung lament. Some advance notice of this kind of plan will be wise so that those who know they would benefit from this kind of lament can try to be there. It also means that those who have experienced trauma and think they would find this difficult can make sure to avoid this church service, or, at the least, step out for the part involving the lament (or know they have the option of doing so easily).

It will also be wise to decide what kind of support will be offered following this kind of corporate lament. Will there be a prayer team or a pastoral care team immediately available at the end of the service? Perhaps, where a small group has already been supporting an individual who has experienced trauma, they will decide to put a specific plan in place both to pray with and support someone for whom this kind of corporate lament could be important. But since lament is a way that we process pain that is oriented to God without minimising the suffering, these are questions well worth wrestling with, to ensure that, so far as we can, we are giving space and time that enables those who have much to lament to do so within the safety and love of a church family.

Questions for reflection

1. What do you think people might find difficult about the process of lament? What feelings do you have about expressing yourself in this way?

2. Why is it important that people are given permission to choose whether or not they participate in lament with others?

3. If you are part of a small group, how would you describe your feelings about including lament as part of a small-group meeting?

CHAPTER 13

TRAUMA AND BEAUTY[61]

The theme of beauty may not, at first sight, seem the most obvious avenue to explore in relation to the experience of trauma. Yet it proves to be not only a powerful lens through which to view the experience of trauma but also a biblical one. For some people, reflections on beauty may provide a powerful source of healing and hope in their journey towards recovery.

The ugliness of our world

Trauma is ugly. Ugliness is the mangled metal of a car accident. It is the angry, abusive parents whose actions toward their children seem set to extinguish every glimmer of joy and hopefulness. It is the brutality of war. It is the protracted illness that slowly distorts a body and erodes a soul. Trauma is ugly.

Whenever trauma enters a life, ugliness intrudes with it. And the origin of all this ugliness is found in the distorting and ruinous impacts of sin. The opening chapters of the Bible describe how God's good and beautiful creation is corrupted by sin. In Genesis 1, God surveys his creation and declares it "very good" (v 31). By Genesis 4, as we've seen, beauty has given way to ugliness as Cain murders his brother, Abel and Lamech, glories in the excesses of violent retribution.

---

61 I am indebted to Todd Stryd and Eamon Wilson for their presentations at the CCEF National Conference in 2023. Their teaching introduced me to the way in which the biblical theme of beauty can speak so powerfully in the context of trauma.

We rightly identify this ugliness as a manifestation of evil. The words with which the serpent lured Eve sounded so appealing, even alluring. But there was ugliness in those words because they distorted the beautiful truth God had spoken. And, once the man and woman had been so tragically deceived, "the eyes of both of them were opened, and they realised that they were naked; so they sewed fig leaves together and made coverings for themselves" (Genesis 3:7). A beautiful honesty and openness gives way to the ugliness of shame and the desire to hide. Sin and evil attacks everything that is beautiful and brings what is ugly in its place.

In this post-fall world, ugliness is everywhere. Ugliness even comes *out of* us—with angry words we hurt those closest to us. With lies and deceit we undermine trust that has been so hard-won. Ugliness distorts the relationships that matter the most to us.

Ugliness also comes *at* us. The ugliness of a premature death or an acrimonious divorce or of vindictive bullying that persists for years. When anger and deceit assail us, we experience what it is to be on the receiving end of that which is ugly.

Ugliness takes hold

When trauma brings ugliness into a person's life, the impact is often far-reaching. Threat brings fearfulness and a desperate attempt to retreat from the ugliness. Isolation follows. When relationships start to feel ugly and threatening, a person will retreat from those too. Lost trust and lost intimacy are the result. Once someone's future only seems to offer more ugliness, they can see nothing to look forward to. Despair follows. The world doesn't look right—nothing looks right. It all looks distorted and dangerous.

Ugliness gets inside, intruding to the very heart of a person. A person to whom ugly things have happened feels contaminated by that ugliness. They often believe themselves to be ugly. When they dare look inside, they may well hate what they see. And with that comes shame.

Once inside, the ugliness continues to assault a person. The intrusions of trauma—the nightmares and the flashbacks—attack them from within. With these recurrences, ugliness asserts its hold until every part of their heart and mind and body feels contaminated by ugliness.

The powerful word of beauty

If ugliness involves distortion and disruption such that things fall apart, beauty proves to be the opposite. Beauty is perfectly proportioned. Beauty has things just as they should be. Beauty holds everything perfectly in place.

This points to the reality that beauty must, ultimately, be found in the one who is perfection itself and in whom all things hold together. Beauty not only comes from God but is finally found in God. Psalm 27 captures the deepest longing of all of us, whether we realise it or not—to see beauty by seeing the face of God himself:

> *"One thing I ask from the LORD,*
> *   this only do I seek:*
> *that I may dwell in the house of the LORD*
> *   all the days of my life,*
> *to gaze on the beauty of the LORD*
> *   and to seek him in his temple.*
> *For in the day of trouble*
> *   he will keep me safe in his dwelling;*
> *he will hide me in the shelter of his sacred tent*
> *   and set me high upon a rock." (Psalm 27:4-5)*

The psalmist longs to be with the Lord in his house and gaze upon him. There is no greater loss than to have the Lord turn his face away from us. And there is no greater blessing than to know the gracious welcome of his smile.

> *"My heart says of you, 'Seek his face!'*
> *Your face, LORD, I will seek.*
> *Do not hide your face from me,*
> *do not turn your servant away in anger;*
> *you have been my helper.*
> *Do not reject me or forsake me,*
> *God my Saviour.*
> *Though my father and mother forsake me,*
> *the LORD will receive me." (v 8-10)*

The Lord is beauty. There is beauty in what he is and there is beauty in whatever he does. And this beauty is good. Something in us knows that. And nothing that God has done is more beautiful than his work of redemption. Even the feet of those who bring this good news are beautiful (Romans 10:15; Isaiah 52:7)! This is because the gospel message that they bring reflects the perfect beauty of God's gracious character. Redemption is beautiful. Grace is beautiful. Heaven will be eternally beautiful.

And for those whose lives have been marred by the ugliness of trauma, this promise of beauty can be life-changing.

Speaking beauty

Psalm 27 captures the restoring impact that comes through an encounter with the beauty of the Lord.

- Fear is overtaken by trust:

> *"The LORD is my light and my salvation—*
> *whom shall I fear?*
> *The LORD is the stronghold of my life—*
> *of whom shall I be afraid? ...*
> *Though an army besiege me,*
> *my heart will not fear;*

though war break out against me,
even then I will be confident." (v 1, 3)

- Despair is overcome by hope:

"I remain confident of this:
I will see the goodness of the LORD
in the land of the living.
Wait for the LORD;
be strong and take heart
and wait for the LORD." (v 13-14)

- Lost intimacy is replaced by the closeness of the living God:

"Though my father and mother forsake me,
the LORD will receive me." (v 10)

- Even shame is taken away as the believer is welcomed into the very presence of God:

"Then my head will be exalted
above the enemies who surround me;
at his sacred tent I will sacrifice with shouts
of joy;
I will sing and make music to the LORD."
(v 6)

Beauty and worship

Central to our experience of worship is coming together to share in a corporate encounter with beauty. We read Bible truth that reminds us of the beauty of our God, and we respond by singing his praises and adoring him in his beauty. We hear the beautiful promises of redeeming grace and declare our faith in that good news. In a world marred by ugliness, we gather as God's people to remind one another that there is a God who is beautiful and who has committed himself to make us beautiful too. God's commitment to the sanctification of his people is a promise that he will form in us the "unfading beauty of a gentle and quiet spirit" (1 Peter 3:4). A day will come when we will be presented to him "as a bride beautifully dressed for her husband" (Revelation 21:2).

Beauty and trauma recovery

Recovering a sense of beauty takes time. Ugliness is not easily expelled from the life of those affected by trauma. But if that journey is to be made, it will be made through an encounter with the one who came to make beauty known. Jesus, as we have seen already, and will spend time dwelling upon more in the next chapter, took the ugliness of a traumatic death upon himself. In his death, an ugly brutality was inflicted upon Jesus so that as sin enveloped him, even the beautiful face of his Father was hidden from him. But all these things happened "so that in him we might become the righteousness of God" (2 Corinthians 5:21). Those who encounter this act of saving grace discover that although the cross seems appallingly ugly, it is, in fact, beauty itself: the beauty of a redeeming death that demonstrates to us the boundless love of God (Romans 5:8). When we encounter this beauty, it forms beauty in us and draws beauty from us. Through an encounter with the redeeming work of Jesus, the ugliness of trauma can begin to be undone.

Restored by beauty

There are many accounts in the Gospels of people being restored—of people who, as they encountered Jesus, were met with grace and liberated from the confines of sin. In each of these descriptions, we see ugliness giving way to beauty. As Jesus put it to the messengers sent by John the Baptist, "Go back and report to John what you hear and see: The blind receive sight, the lame walk, those who have leprosy are cleansed, the deaf hear, the dead are raised, and the good news is proclaimed to the poor. Blessed is anyone who does not stumble on account of me" (Matthew 11:4-6). Jesus brings the beauty of a restored humanity.

One person who knew that restoration was the woman described in Mark 14. She came to Jesus and not only anointed his feet with perfume but dried his feet with her hair. Here is a woman so captured by the beauty of Jesus that she is drawn to respond with the most extravagant demonstration of love. It is a demonstration that Jesus declares to be filled with beauty. The onlookers disapprove, believing it would have been better if the perfume had been sold and the money given to the poor. But Jesus will have none of this: "Leave her alone ... She has done a beautiful thing to me" (v 6). This woman has experienced beauty in the grace extended to her by Christ, and she has responded by doing something beautiful to him.

The way that encountering the beauty of Jesus transforms us, even when we are struggling with the ugliness of trauma, is (beautifully!) captured in Isaiah:

> "The Spirit of the Sovereign LORD is on me,
>   because the Lord has anointed me
>   to proclaim good news to the poor.
> He has sent me to bind up the broken-hearted,
>   to proclaim freedom for the captives
>   and release from darkness for the prisoners,
> to proclaim the year of the LORD's favour
>   and the day of vengeance of our God,
> to comfort all who mourn,
>   and provide for those who grieve in Zion—
> to bestow on them a crown of beauty
>   instead of ashes,

the oil of joy
  instead of mourning,
and a garment of praise
  instead of a spirit of despair.
They will be called oaks of righteousness,
  a planting of the LORD
  for the display of his splendour." (v 1-3)

Helping others through beauty

There are many ways that these themes of ugliness and beauty might guide the support and care we offer to those who have experienced trauma.

Again, first of all, there is the need to listen—to acknowledge the ugliness of what has happened to someone. Chaos and disruption may be prominent results of trauma, and it can be helpful to verbalise these impacts. It may be important to focus on the ugly actions of another person, naming the damage their actions have caused.

Secondly, passages that describe and declare the beauty of the Lord can lift a person's eyes from the ugliness of the past to gaze upon their Saviour. Revelation 1:12-16 and Job 38 – 39 are passages that capture the majesty and glory of God. Many psalms also depict a vision of the loveliness of God—Psalms 104, 111, 113, 136 and 145 to name just a few. Reading and reflecting on these psalms and inviting a time of adoration—declaring the excellence and beauty of God—can be a helpful way to encourage someone to engage with beauty in place of ugliness.

Thirdly, when we gather as God's people together, there are many ways that we can turn our focus onto the beauty of God. It can happen in the simplicity of the public or corporate reading of a psalm. It can happen when listening to a song of worship, beautifully performed by others. It can happen as we join in such sung worship with others.

It can happen in words of testimony as a believer describes the beautiful way the Lord has cared for them and has used God's people in that care. It can happen in sharing bread and wine, as the beauty of God's love demonstrated in the sacrifice of Christ is remembered again. It can happen in the beauty of a liturgy of thanksgiving and praise.

Any of these aspects of our corporate worship can direct our gaze away from the ugliness we may have experienced, or may be experiencing, to behold the beauty of our God. All may be used by God in the ordinary (and not at all ordinary) practices of the worshipping people of God. That these things are done in community brings with it the experience of the deepening and slowly increasing beauty of the body of Christ.

Finally, there is a beauty that is found in service. There is something good and right and coherent in giving ourselves in service to others. Serving someone who has experienced trauma offers them a glimpse of beauty—and to then encourage them, gently, to return to active service in the body of Christ can be hugely restorative.

In its ugliness, trauma disrupts, isolates and destroys. Serving others is an almost direct antithesis to this. Serving builds—it builds relationships, builds community and builds a sense of value both in the one who serves and the one who is served. It feels right and good to serve. In that sense, it helps to restore a sense of the beauty and goodness of life—and a glimpse of the ultimate and eternal beauty of the one who came not to be served but to serve.

Questions for reflection

1. Can you recall a time when have you been especially aware of the beauty of the Lord?

2. It takes time to properly appreciate beauty. In what ways could you give more time to the contemplation of the beauty of the Lord? How could you help others do this?

3. Since we need to see beauty ourselves before we can share it with others, what will help you to experience more of the Lord's beauty?

CHAPTER 14

TRAUMA AND THE HOPE OF JESUS CHRIST

In the ugliness of trauma, beauty intrudes—and that beauty is most fully and wonderfully encountered in the person of Jesus Christ. As we lament, we begin to hope—and Jesus provides the ultimate hope to which lament points.

As we consider how the redemption that Christ brings helps us to walk alongside those struggling with trauma, two things are needed. First of all, we can joyfully and confidently proclaim that whatever trauma a person may face, Christ provides the redeeming love they need. Yet second, we must do this in a way that does not end up implying that there is anything simple or easy about grasping and living in response to the redemption Christ provides. Trauma's impact is not quickly resolved. Growth in Christ is something that is gradual and lifelong—and we need to bring a similar mindset to the process of recovery from trauma. No one sees all the beauty of Christ in an instant. It will take more than a lifetime to fully comprehend the work of Christ for us. It also takes more than a lifetime to fully respond in love and devotion to him.

But nevertheless, it is to Jesus that we need to bring our friends who are suffering.

Christ knows our suffering

As we've seen, trauma isolates a person. It damages their relationships. Someone who has lived through trauma often feels that no one does, or ever could, fully understand what they have been through. It feels as if no one can really be with them in their struggles. The particular experience of their suffering leaves them profoundly alone.

But in every sense and in the deepest way, Jesus does understand. The God who became man is neither far off nor detached from those who suffer. The Christian doctrine of the incarnation is enormously significant for those who suffer trauma. It tells them that in Christ God has entered into this world—that he knows.

> *"Since the children have flesh and blood, he too shared*
> *in their humanity so that by his death he might break*
> *the power of him who holds the power of death—that*
> *is, the devil— and free those who all their lives were*
> *held in slavery by their fear of death."*
>
> *(Hebrews 2:14-15)*

Definitions of trauma often emphasise death coming near and the terror that arrives with it. Hebrews tells us that in order to break the power of death, Christ came and shared our humanity. He knows what it is to be flesh and blood. He knows what it is to suffer. "The God on whom we rely knows what suffering is all about, not merely in the way that God knows everything, but by experience."[62]

A woman who had suffered the violence of domestic abuse had this to say about the death of Jesus: "This cross story ... it's the only part of this Christian thing I like. I get it. And, it's like he gets me. He knows."[63] The experience of trauma threatens to isolate a person, but the cross of Jesus tells them that, however awful their suffering, ultimately they are not alone.

---

62 D.A. Carson, *How Long, O Lord? Reflections on Suffering and Evil* (Baker, 1990), p. 179.
63 Quoted in *Trauma and Grace*, p. 76.

Christ takes our suffering

The incarnation is, however, about something much more than simply having a God who understands our human experience. And the cross is about something more than a mere demonstration of solidarity with our suffering. Tim Keller's vivid language captures the significance of the incarnation vividly when he says that in taking on flesh, Jesus wasn't simply making God visible; he was also making God killable.[64] Christ came to take our suffering—to bear God's wrath against sin and to taste the spiritual death of hell in our place. He endured that suffering and that death as our substitute:

> *"He suffered death, so that by the grace of God he might taste death for everyone." (Hebrews 2:9)*

> *"Christ also suffered once for sins, the righteous for the unrighteous, to bring you to God." (1 Peter 3:18)*

On the cross Jesus seemed helpless in the face of suffering. "'He saved others,' they said, 'but he can't save himself!'" (Matthew 27:42). Yet in reality this suffering was something Jesus chose to endure. Indeed, Jesus told Pontius Pilate that despite him being the Roman governor, "you would have no power over me if it were not given to you from above" (John 19:11). Jesus was handed over to suffering "by God's deliberate plan and foreknowledge" (Acts 2:23). He chose to suffer, and in so doing took the worst suffering imaginable in our place, so that we need never experience it.

Christ ends our suffering

The cross speaks of a glorious exchange. There was a traumatic death for Christ. There was freedom from sin and

---

64 facebook.com/TimKellerNYC/posts/jesus-became-killable-out-of-love-for-us/679707166844325/ (accessed 14th August 2024).

death for us. At the cross Jesus won the victory over death and sin and evil. Trauma is often an experience where evil enters into a person's life. Sometimes that is the impersonal evil of a broken and ruined world; on other occasions the evil is all too personal. To someone who has endured terrible evil at another's hands, the defeat of evil, secured at the cross, and seen when Jesus returns in judgment, salvation and restoration, is a precious truth.

Virtually every kind of sin and violence and injustice imaginable was thrown at Jesus. It was the worst that could be done. And yet the outpouring of that evil proved to be its very undoing:

> *"At the cross evil is conquered as evil ... evil is*
> *conquered as evil because God turns it back upon itself.*
> *He makes the supreme crime, the murder of the only*
> *righteous person, the very operation that abolishes sin*
> *... No more complete victory could be imagined ...*
> *God entraps the deceiver in his own wiles."*[65]

Trauma often involves overwhelming violence being inflicted on a person. This violence cuts across all the normal boundaries that we use to keep ourselves safe and to protect ourselves from harm. It is striking, therefore, that in his rescue, Christ also steps across boundaries. He spans the very divide that exists between creation and Creator. He enters in. He reaches us in our need.

This is also happening, in a limited way, whenever a helper reaches out to someone who has suffered trauma and crosses the barriers that have left them isolated. Such help is an echo of the remedy found in the cross. By submitting himself to the agonies of the cross, Jesus was reaching across

---

65 Henri Blocher, *Evil and the Cross*, quoted in Timothy Keller, *Walking with God through Pain and Suffering* (Hodder and Stoughton, 2013), p. 157.

the spiritual barriers that isolate every one of us. In doing so, he has brought about the promise of an ultimate victory. A victory that defeats every evil and will set aside both suffering and death. For the believer this is a comfort that is experienced in part, and in anticipation, now. But our comfort is that it will be experienced in full and ultimate glory in eternity.

A sufferer restored

In Mark 5, Jesus was approached by that woman "who had been subject to bleeding for twelve years. She had suffered a great deal under the care of many doctors and had spent all she had, yet instead of getting better she grew worse" (Mark 5:25-26).

She approached Jesus from behind, convinced that if she just touched his clothes, she would be healed. And so it turned out. But Jesus, realising that "power had gone out from him" (v 30), was determined to discover who it was who had touched his clothes. There is something strange about this. The woman, it seems, was keen to avoid identification. Her bleeding would have made her ceremonially unclean. Even being present in the crowd may have involved a breach of religious rules.

When she did eventually reveal herself, she was "trembling with fear" (v 33). It seems odd that Jesus forced this exposure. He could have let her depart unnoticed—instead he insisted that she identify herself. Why?

There are probably several answers to that question. One possibility, however, is that he wanted something more for her than simply physical healing. Once Jesus had summoned her out into the open, he declared both her healing and her restoration. He restored her, not just to physical health but also into the body of the community. This woman, who had been known for her unclean bleeding, was now known for her health and healing. Jesus restored her to the community from which she had become an outcast.

Hebrews 12:2 speaks of the way that Jesus, "for the joy that was set before him ... endured the cross, scorning its shame". It is not only that the cross was a shameful way to die, but also that, on the cross, Jesus took all the guilt of every wrong. He took on the shame and guilt of our world—every evil action—and also delivered perfect justice. The cross removes the cloak of shame and covers us in robes of righteousness. He declares us as his beloved and as beautiful in his eyes.

Restoration from trauma is neither quick nor easy. The grace and the work of the cross do not bring an instant remedy to every present-day struggle. It would be wrong to promise such a thing to those whose lives have been affected by trauma. Yet there is both the promise of ultimate restoration and the beginning of transformation in the present too, and it would be equally wrong not to keep pointing sufferers to this truth.

The cross of Jesus is the basis for hope in the lives of those who have faced extreme suffering. It is Christ's victory over evil and suffering. It provides a pattern to follow as those who offer help draw close to those who feel far off and as they offer Christ-like sacrificial love. And wonderfully, it holds out to us the glorious promise of a new heaven and a new earth, where righteousness dwells (2 Peter 3:13). That is the promise we can hold out to those who have been burdened by the brokenness of this world.

Questions for reflection

1. How do you make sense of Jesus' decision to draw out into the open the woman who touched his clothes in Mark 5?

2. Perhaps you are familiar with the idea that in his death on the cross, Jesus conquered sin and death, but think rather less about the cross meaning that one day there will be an end to suffering—why would that mean so much to someone who has experienced trauma?

3. A woman unfamiliar with the Christian faith who had suffered domestic abuse said that the cross was "the only part of this Christian thing I like. I get it. And, it's like he gets me. He knows." What do you think it was about the cross that this woman valued so much?

CHAPTER 15

CHURCHES THAT CARE WELL

Not many of our churches—and not many of us individually—will feel that we have expertise in the care of those who have suffered trauma. The very nature of trauma can leave us feeling overwhelmed. We can't see what difference our contribution is going to make. Our limited, far from expert input seems so insubstantial in the face of the trauma that someone has faced.

Yet we can make a difference. And it's not necessary to be experts to do so. We can learn to offer thoughtful, compassionate care to those who have faced trauma, and we can resolve to persevere in that care even when people's struggles persist. Any church can demonstrate humility by being willing to listen to those affected by trauma and adapt its care accordingly.

We cannot fix everyone's problems, and that's not what we are called to do. We can persist in compassionate care; we can persist in holding out hope and love; we can persist in pointing people to Christ, and we can persist in praying. A community that does these things, in reliance on the Spirit, has something very powerful and very significant to offer.

Caring for Morten

Remember Morten, who we met in chapter 3? He was the man who had been mugged and was now experiencing anxiety about going out, especially at night. It had badly affected his efforts to attend a small group in his new church, and his small-group leaders, Ben and Niko, had largely given up on him. Happily, things took a turn for the better.

Almost a year after Ben and Niko had last been in touch with Morten, Ben noticed a small news item in their local paper. It concerned the prosecution of a man for mugging, and one of the victims identified was Morten. The police had found items belonging to Morten in this man's possession, and this had led to the prosecution.

It prompted Ben to send Morten a handwritten note, and, as he wrote, something prompted him to tentatively ask whether this mugging was connected in any way with Morten's anxieties about getting to home group. Ben ended the letter with these words: "Morten, if this horrible experience is, in any way, connected with the struggles you experienced in getting to the home group last year, then can I say that I am really sorry. I am sorry that we didn't think to ask more questions about those struggles, and I am sorry that we didn't make more effort to reach out and care for you. Please know that whether these things are connected or not, we care about you and want to do whatever we can to support you, regardless of any involvement with the home group here."

When Morten got the letter, it moved him to tears. Suddenly, Morten realised just how isolated and misunderstood he had been feeling. To receive Ben's letter and to have him extend an apology like that seemed truly wonderful. Morten didn't actually blame Ben and Niko. How could they have known what was going on? He had always felt he should probably have told them, but felt too ashamed of it all. To have Ben show understanding meant so much.

Soon Morten had met up with Ben and Niko and filled in the background in a bit more detail. They didn't press him for details—in fact they said that he mustn't feel under any pressure to talk—but they did listen carefully to what he chose to tell them and seemed really sympathetic. They mentioned a book they had been reading about lament and asked what Morten thought about taking time to read a lament and pray together one evening. Morten had never thought much about lamenting, but when they described what they had in mind, it seemed to make sense.

A week or two later, they sat down to look at Psalm 17 together. There was nothing complicated about the evening. They read the psalm and each said a little bit about what had struck them from it. Morten was especially struck by verses 11-12:

> *"They have tracked me down, they now surround me,*
> *with eyes alert, to throw me to the ground.*
> *They are like a lion hungry for prey,*
> *like a fierce lion crouching in cover."*

It almost felt like that was describing what had happened to him, and he felt comforted by the realisation that an experience that had done him so much damage was reflected like this in the Bible.

He also noticed verses 6-9:

> *"I call on you, my God, for you will answer me;*
> *turn your ear to me and hear my prayer.*
> *Show me the wonders of your great love,*
> *you who save by your right hand*
> *those who take refuge in you from their foes.*
> *Keep me as the apple of your eye;*
> *hide me in the shadow of your wings*
> *from the wicked who are out to destroy me,*
> *from my mortal enemies who surround me."*

It was a precious thought to remember that, in Christ, he was the apple of God's eye. It was also precious to remember that he could call on God to show the wonders of his great love, and, in a small but very significant way, the evening he was spending with Ben and Niko felt like an expression of that great love. He felt cared for and welcomed in a way that he couldn't remember having felt since the mugging took place.

Morten's fears about going out didn't vanish. Some weeks he still couldn't bring himself to venture out, but now when he messaged the group to tell them, he felt understood and supported. They would reassure him that they understood, would pray for him, and were always ready to discuss things that might help him when the anxieties mounted.

One significant step forward came when the whole home group spent an evening looking at Psalm 17 together. What was special about that evening was how it wasn't focused on Morten. He was surprised to find that, in response to the psalm, many in the group began to talk about their own struggles: about difficulties that they hadn't, till that point, felt able to describe. Afterwards Ben and Niko comment- ed to Morten that it seemed as if God was using Morten's struggles to help others in the group be honest about their own. They observed that the group felt more close-knit now than at any point since they had started leading.

Morten still struggles with anxieties, but he feels loved and understood now in ways he hadn't done, even before the mugging. He can also begin to see how something that has been so very hard and damaging is also something that God is using for good—and that is a comfort to him too.

Caring for Naomi

Naomi, as you may remember, had emailed a church office to ask for a meeting with someone in the church leadership. The oddness of her request was that she had asked for a list of people to choose from and requested that the meeting take place away from the church building. The reason for those strange requests was the extended abuse that had been inflicted on her by the church minister who had led her to Christ. The email she sent was her first step in an attempt to re-engage with church after that experience of abuse.

Both Aisha, the office administrator, and the pastor to whom she had shown it found the email distinctly odd. A week had passed, and Aisha was pretty sure the pastor had forgotten he was supposed to be deciding how to reply. She was just about to delete the email when a verse from her morning Bible study popped into her mind. The passage had been Isaiah 42, and the devotional book she was reading had reflected on the different ways that a person can be a "bruised reed" and on the loveliness of Jesus' care for all such people.

It set Aisha wondering. What if the strange email came from someone who was in some way a bruised reed? Perhaps this wasn't someone who was difficult and demanding but someone who was really struggling and was reaching out in the only way she could? She decided to try and get more information, and, distractedly, the pastor said it was fine for her to follow it up herself. Aisha hadn't anticipated that Naomi, rather than explain herself by email, would ask to talk on the phone. There was enough in that conversation for Aisha to realise that her suspicion that Naomi might be a broken reed was only too accurate.

Aisha immediately felt way out of her depth but, crucially for Naomi, Aisha didn't back away. She asked if Naomi might be willing to meet with Christine, a woman on the church's pastoral staff. She could hear Naomi hesitate so found herself saying that, if it would help, she could be there as well. That offer proved crucial.

From Naomi's perspective, there was something in Aisha's initial email that gave her confidence to proceed. Even though it was only brief, it communicated generosity, and that made Naomi feel able to talk. In the phone conversation with Aisha, Naomi felt listened to. Aisha was just being herself. There was no rigid following of procedures, and she never tried to tell Naomi what to do. She just listened and seemed to want to understand.

That said, when Aisha suggested a meeting with the pastoral worker, Naomi almost backed away. But Aisha's offer to also be present at the meeting, and her assurance that it could happen away from the church building, helped Naomi go through with it. When she met with Christine, Naomi was able to give an outline of her previous church experience but didn't feel under any pressure to go into detail. Then Christine asked what they, as a church, could do to be most helpful. That question alone grew trust. She said she didn't want, at this point, to explain everything that had happened, but that she did want to try and get back into church.

Together they formed a plan. Christine suggested that Naomi come to the church building midweek when there would be few people around. They met in a local café and walked to the building together. It was incredibly stressful, but Christine's calm and reassuring presence helped her keep going. They did that a few times and then discussed how she might manage a Sunday service. The welcome team were forewarned. They weren't given any detail—just told that Naomi would find it hard to be in church and that they should be welcoming but leave Christine to care for her.

Much to Naomi's surprise, within a few weeks she was managing to get to church on her own. She still sits at the back, and the welcome team know to look out for her and always make sure no one crowds her or obstructs the exit. It's early days, but the flexibility and understanding that has already been shown has made such a difference to her sense of trust in the church.

Of course, things haven't all been plain sailing. At one

point, someone tried to move Naomi out of her chair at the back and told her that it was important for her to be part of the body of Christ and not separate herself from others. She was on the point of fleeing when someone from the welcome team saw what was happening and intervened.

It so happened that on one of the first Sundays that Naomi was in church, the sermon was from that same passage in Isaiah 42. The preacher made much of the "bruised reed" verse. He said churches needed to be communities that reflected the compassion and gentleness of Christ. His prayer at the end was all about God helping them to be just such a community.

At various points Naomi's fears and flashbacks have nearly been enough to make her give up. But there is something about this church's determination to be a compassionate community in imitation of Christ that keeps drawing her back. They haven't just spoken to her of the love of Christ; they have demonstrated it too. And they have consistently prayed for her whenever she has begun to struggle. So far, that has pointed her to Christ and been what she needs to keep her going.

The God of all comfort

Every act of compassion echoes the compassion of Christ. And no act of compassion is greater than the one that takes a person to the demonstration of Christ's love upon the cross.

> *"Praise be to the God and Father of our Lord Jesus Christ, the Father of compassion and the God of all comfort, who comforts us in all our troubles, so that we can comfort those in any trouble with the comfort we ourselves receive from God." (2 Corinthians 1:3-4)*

APPENDIX

CONCERNING BEING "TRAUMA AWARE", CONCEPT CREEP, AND CONTRARY VOICES

Christians who want to communicate the gospel have always recognised the need to understand their hearers. In Acts 17 Paul surveyed the attitudes of the Athenians (v 16, 22-23) before delivering his message to the Areopagus. Today a cross-cultural church planter will work hard to understand the local culture before embarking on ministry. This careful listening is not in order that we might adapt the gospel to fit but about determining how we can most accurately and effectively communicate the truth about Jesus Christ. The language, stories and illustrations we use will, rightly, vary both from person to person and from culture to culture.

Western culture's awareness of trauma has increased greatly in recent years. When social commentators suggest "trauma" as the word of the decade, it is clear that this is an experience that many are thinking and talking about. In other words, it is now part of the thought framework and language of our culture—of the people around us with whom we want to share the gospel and the people in our churches (including ourselves) who are wanting to base their lives on the gospel.

We all know how words and phrases that seem innocuous in one context can land very awkwardly in another. Being "trauma informed" has become a much-used term, and it means different things to different people. It may not be the most helpful phrase, but at its simplest, it means being aware that trauma is a lens through which many people view the world. Learning what this perspective means for them is both wise and loving. This chapter brings together some broader reflections about how we can understand and respond well in relation to trauma.

Understanding suffering

Trauma studies have helped identify some of the ways that severe suffering can impact a person. Some of these effects are reasonably intuitive, but by no means all. We considered the idea of dissociation earlier. Writing about her work with people who have been diagnosed with complex PTSD, Heather Davediuk Gingrich comments that "perhaps the biggest stumbling block for churches is a lack of understanding about [complex PTSD] and dissociation. Highly dissociative individuals are at increased risk of being misunderstood by other Christians."[66] This does not mean that those most directly involved in church pastoral care need to become experts in psychological terminology or to have the capacity to deliver the kinds of interventions used by secular therapists. But they should be aware of just how extensive the personal disturbance caused by trauma can sometimes be.

Knowing something about these ongoing effects of trauma also helps to raise our levels of compassion. We might not, otherwise, appreciate how far-reaching the impact of suffering can be. The precision of our compassion will also change. Knowing more clearly what it is that a person is experiencing enables us to direct our care and

---

66 *Restoring the Shattered Self: A Christian Counselor's Guide to Complex Trauma* (IVP US, 2020), p. 215.

support more accurately. We can listen more attentively, care more thoughtfully and pray more specifically.

Preachers who are familiar with the impact of trauma will also be more precise when their preaching addresses experiences of severe suffering. That, in turn, will help to create a church culture that is more receptive to such struggles. Gingrich is again helpful here: "Pastors can be encouraged to preach on topics that address the issues that those with [complex PTSD] face. For example, sermons that address the evils of abuse, acknowledge the reality of suffering, and encourage individuals to seek answers to hard questions can give trauma survivors permission to be more open about their struggles."[67]

Speaking gospel hope

In one of his many vivid metaphors, David Powlison used the imagery of Velcro to emphasise the struggle we sometimes find as we try to bring God's word to bear upon a person's struggles: "You grope to bridge the disconnect. Perhaps you earnestly rehearse the right answers, but the Velcro hooks of the Word find no Velcro loops in a slippery soul. The sweet light has no effect on bitter darkness."[68]

When someone feels that we haven't properly understood their struggle, they will often find it hard to hear our words of hope. Our "right answers" keep missing them. The gospel words we speak may be true and accurate, but they seem to lack connection. Somewhere in the background, it is as if the person is saying, "That's all very good, but you just don't seem to understand what it is that I am going through".

---

67 As above, p. 217.
68 "Think Globally, Act Locally" in *Journal of Biblical Counseling* 22:1 (2003), p. 2.

Most pastoral encounters begin with what we might call "felt needs", and the person who has endured severe suffering feels many needs—their struggles are very real. Without an understanding of the experience of severe suffering, we will always struggle to meet people where they are. And without that starting point, it will always be hard to move forward together.

If being "trauma aware" means being better able to understand severe suffering, better able to apply God's word in that experience and better able to welcome and care for those who struggle in this way, then it is not just a sensible ambition; it is also a deeply gospel-hearted one.

The broadening (and trivialising) of trauma

Trauma moving from the margins to the forefront of thinking and writing in the mental-health field has been positive in many ways—people whose experiences had been ignored and misunderstood have begun to receive the attention and care they need.

Continuing studies will, in all probability, bring new insights. And these new insights will, no doubt, lead to new treatments being developed. The wide range of approaches currently available in the field of "trauma therapy" suggests we are still in a period of transition. At present the category of "trauma" functions something like an umbrella term and includes many different experiences. As this field develops, there is likely to be a further delineation of separate sub-categories of trauma.

Acute, chronic and complex trauma are already widely recognised categories. Other sub-types are also emerging, such as childhood developmental trauma, collective trauma (something experienced by a large number of people simultaneously), and intergenerational trauma. The related concept of moral injury has been used to describe what happens when someone undergoes an experience that is contrary to their moral beliefs. Military personnel, for example, would suffer a moral injury if they were forced to follow orders which were contrary to their own moral code. Other researchers use the concept of moral injury to describe the experience of being caught up in a work environment that a person believes to be morally wrong but where they feel powerless to bring about change. For example, health personnel with an excessive workload might feel unable to deliver the standard of care they consider adequate—this would lead them to feel a moral injury.

The continuing expansion of trauma research and therapy will produce many positive benefits. However, the law of unintended consequences is always at work. Positive advances will sit alongside developments that are less constructive. Without wanting to set aside the many positives already explored, certain concerns are also being identified.

We've noted how the language of "trauma" is increasingly used in popular culture to describe events which are little more than mild inconveniences. A cancelled train or a drenching rain shower used to be annoying. Now they can be the reason for someone to declare, "I've had such a traumatic morning". One opinion piece comments that in today's culture, references to trauma have become "a mess of tongue-in-cheek and casual mentions" so that the word risks becoming "a popular idiom tossed around without meaning"[69]—what Nicholas Haslam describes as "concept creep". He believes this has significant implications for the way we manage difficulties in our lives: "Seeing a wide range of common but unpleasant life experiences

---

69 Lexi Pandell, "How trauma became the word of the decade", vox.com/the-highlight/22876522/trauma-covid-word-origin-mental-health (accessed 29th May 2024).

as traumas is simultaneously to flatten out the landscape of life events and to represent all adversities as severe and life-shattering".[70] This has two effects. First, by trivialising the concept of trauma, the word becomes insufficient to describe the experience of those for whom severe suffering has entered their lives. Now that it is being used colloquially for normal life troubles, trauma is no longer a sufficiently weighty word to capture life-altering and "beyond normal experience" events in people's lives.

Second, people may feel themselves more troubled than necessary. When a person thinks of themselves as having experienced "trauma", they may expect difficulties that would not have occurred to them if they had simply faced a "difficult" or an "upsetting" event. "When we describe misfortune, sadness or even pain as trauma, we redefine our experience. Using the word 'trauma' turns every event into a catastrophe, leaving us helpless, broken and unable to move on."[71]

One description sometimes used to characterise the impact of trauma is to say that it can leave a person with a psychological scar. The image conjures up something that is permanent and disfiguring and beyond repair. The more we see life difficulties in terms of "trauma", the more we foster perspectives which view ourselves as having suffered "damage" and as people who are "victims". "Rising sensitivity to harm can shade into hyper-sensitivity … Perceiving challenging life experiences as traumas may therefore increase our vulnerability to them."[72]

---

70 Haslam, N. & McGrath, M.J. "The Creeping Concept of Trauma" in Social Research: An International Quarterly 91(1) (2024), p. 311-334.

71 Nicholas Haslam, "How we became a country where bad hair days and campaign signs cause 'trauma'" in The Washington Post, washingtonpost.com/posteverything/wp/2016/08/12/when-bad-hair-days-and-campaign-signs-cause-trauma-the-concept-has-gone-too-far/ (accessed 7th August 2024).

72 As above.

Hearing critique but maintaining compassion

We have already identified some of the cautions that are felt in relation to the expanding field of trauma studies. The casual use of "trauma" language is one such concern. Others take exception to the terminology being used to describe the impact of severe suffering. Still others question the usefulness of the models that seek to explain the "mechanisms" underlying the features seen in trauma.

The language used to describe these experiences can certainly make them sound unfamiliar and slightly mysterious. It can also make it harder to connect them to the Bible's perspective on suffering. The language of trauma and the language of Scripture can seem dislocated from one another. When they are regarded in that way, Christians are at risk either of unthinkingly accepting contemporary thinking or of unthinkingly rejecting it. More work is needed to identify the connections between contemporary studies of trauma and the theological framework of the Scriptures.

Although trauma theories are now widely used as explanatory models, it should be noted that some writers have questioned the reliability of the scientific studies behind them. An assessment of that critique is beyond the scope of this book. But dissenting voices do exist.[73]

All these different concerns deserve attention. They must not, however, cause us to be dismissive of (or even seem to be dismissive of) the impact that trauma can have. The driver for our response must be compassion—a Christlike care for those who have endured suffering. In that compassion, we will want to offer the greatest gift that we have at our disposal, which is the love of Christ himself.

Christ entered our world to set aside sin and suffering. His work of salvation was accomplished through the suffering of

---

73 Michael Scheeringa, *The Trouble with Trauma* (Central Recovery Press, 2021)

the cross. Whatever new insights may arise concerning the impact of trauma, the one central reality of which we can always be confident is the final victory of Christ over sin and suffering and death.

FURTHER READING

Curtis Solomon, *I Have PTSD* (New Growth Press, 2023)

Darby Strickland, *Trauma: Caring for Survivors* (P&R, 2023)

Darby Strickland, *Is It Abuse?* (P&R, 2020)

Esther Liu, *Shame: Being Known and Loved* (P&R, 2022)

Marcus Honeysett, *Powerful Leaders?* (IVP UK, 2022)

Mez McConnell, *The Creaking on the Stairs* (Christian Focus, 2019)

ACKNOWLEDGEMENTS

I am grateful for the wonderful support I enjoy from my colleagues at Biblical Counselling UK. God has blessed me with a tremendous staff team to work with, and I so appreciate the encouragement they have all shown me during the harder yards of writing this book. I am particularly grateful to Helen Thorne-Allenson, who, as a supremely gifted writer, has always been so wonderfully supportive in her guidance to this newcomer!

I am also so very grateful to God for the many ways I have been blessed through the ministry of CCEF. They remain the most amazingly generous supporters of BCUK. This book, and the ministry I have today, would not exist were it not for the shaping influence of David Powlison upon my life. The hospitality that I enjoyed from David and Nan is precious in my memory.

The church family at Christ Church Cambridge have, over the past 20 years, been the best of congregations to pastor. My understanding of what it means for a community of believers to be the body of Christ has been formed over those years, and I have counted it the greatest privilege to serve there.

As every church minister will tell you, God has taught me so much by allowing me to walk alongside others as their pastor. It has been my very great privilege to minister to people as they have faced, and remembered, their personal experiences of trauma. They have been my teachers and when, at times, I was a slow learner, they were invariably patient. The struggles they have shared with me and the faith they have demonstrated in their suffering are reflected in every one of the imaginary examples I have constructed in these chapters.

Carl Laferton has been a wonderfully calm, thorough and attentive editor. His ability to find better ways of saying things, even in areas with which he felt unfamiliar, was simply exceptional. This is an immeasurably better book as a result of his input, and I am very grateful.

I have also benefited from those who kindly read and commented on early versions of the manuscript. This includes my colleagues Helen Thorne-Allenson and Andrew Collins, as well as Laura Perbet and Karen Sleeman. Their detailed comments added many fresh insights and identified places where I did not express myself clearly. Kenny Larsen was a particular help in improving the chapter on definitions and descriptions. Despite being busy with their own writing, Mike Emlet and Ed Welch also provided much-appreciated feedback and guidance. The final version, however, and whatever errors it still contains, rests with me.

Behind the scenes, Ruth Roberts has provided so much more than administrative support—her calm support and her ability to anticipate what I need to be doing and then helping me get it done has been critical in enabling me to have the time I needed to write this book.

The writing of this book took place in the year after we had moved house and embarked on a building project. That meant the usual dose of disruption. It also meant the arrival of our builders, Jack Moore and Tony O'Mahony, whose good humour and banter with their "project manager" (my good friend Richard Newman) was the very best of light relief as I grappled with heavy writing material.

Finally, and most importantly, I express my tribute and gratitude to my wife, Beth. The depth of her wisdom (on which I regularly rely) and the perseverance of her love (by which I am constantly blessed) are my greatest treasure after Christ. In her I see Christ's passion for those in need and the beauty of grace from which I have learnt so much. I am ever grateful to God for bringing her into my life.

My prayer is that this book would help all of us, in our churches, to glorify God more fully by bringing gospel blessings to those who, in their traumas, have faced the gravest kinds of suffering.

Also by Steve Midgley

This wise, compassionate and practical
book equips readers to make their church
a place where those who struggle with
mental-health conditions are welcomed,
understood, nurtured and supported.

thegoodbook.com/mental-health-book
thegoodbook.co.uk/mental-health-book
thegoodbook.com.au/mental-health-book

COMPANY

BIBLICAL | RELEVANT | ACCESSIBLE

At The Good Book Company we are dedicated to helping Christians and local churches grow. We believe that God's growth process always starts with hearing clearly what he has said to us through his timeless and flawless word—the Bible.

Ever since we opened our doors in 1991, we have been striving to produce resources that are biblical, relevant, and accessible. By God's grace, we have grown to become an international publisher, encouraging ordinary Christians of every age and stage and every background and denomination to live for Christ day by day and equipping churches to grow in their knowledge of God, their love for one another, and the effectiveness of their outreach.

Call one of our friendly team for a discussion of your needs or visit one of our local websites for more information on the resources and services we provide.

Your friends at The Good Book Company

thegoodbook.com | thegoodbook.co.uk
thegoodbook.com.au | thegoodbook.co.nz
thegoodbook.co.in